If GOD doesn't build the house, the builders only build shacks. Psalms 127:1 (Message)

# *Kingdom Engineering*

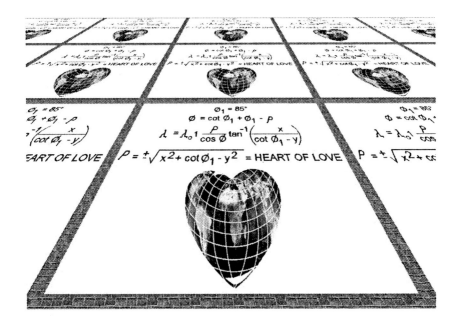

**Taking God to the World Using Engineering Principles**

# Dedication

$\mathcal{B}$efore I get started, I want to acknowledge and celebrate God's provision in giving me the ability to write the thoughts that He planted, and to commit this book to His purpose, which is to increase the glory of His name. I want to thank the Lord, because it is He who has been building my life. I dedicate this book to Him because He found a stone, and made it fit into His purpose by making me, once a dead stone, into a living stone.

I also want to dedicate this book to my lovely wife, Pam, who has supported me and still supports me in every endeavor that I embark upon. I always imagine that if I looked up the words "help mate" in the dictionary, her name should appear there. She is the personification of a helpmate, a talented, intelligent, and a beautiful woman. She sacrificially studied engineering simply to be at my right hand, and to support me in an engineering business endeavor. I say sacrificially because her heart has always been in the spiritual, emotional, and psychological care of others. I believe her to be the world's big sister.

In time, she went back to Liberty University and received a Master's Degree in Christian Counseling. Before now, I could not understand the value of a counselor. After all, as an engineer, if a problem arose, I usually responded with calculations and a set of solutions. I would usually come up with alternative solutions, for I am a problem solver. Unlike me, her approach is to reach the inner heart of man and take it to the Lord in prayer to help those in need. She was very instrumental in the writing of this book, and has made every effort to keep me from writing just another engineering textbook with mathematical equations, and to help me write a book that relates the analytical with the spiritual.

In addition, I dedicate this book to my two sons, Nate and Jonathan, whom I admire profoundly. They are faithful men of God, who serve and love the Lord with all their hearts. They both received and answered the call to serve Him at an early age. They are men who have the fervency to proclaim the Gospel and to utilize many talents that the Lord has imparted upon them.

I am the product of five generations of engineers; generations who have worked on projects like the Suez Canal, Panama Canal, Pan-American Highway, and other heavy civil engineering projects. While I am proud of my lineage, my greatest legacy will be that my sons, Nate and Jonathan, along with their lovely wives, Kelsey and Shannon, proclaim a higher calling, and that is to serve the Lord with all their hearts. I love you all, and I thank you for your steadfast support.

If GOD doesn't build the house, the builders only build shacks. Psalms 127:1 (Message)

# TABLE OF CONTENTS

If GOD doesn't build the house, the builders only build shacks. Psalms 127:1 (Message)

If God doesn't build the house, the builders only build shacks. Psalms 127:1 (Message)

# Foreword

This book has been written in an effort to illustrate particular contents of the Bible from the perspective of an engineer/builder. Engineering is scientific, and the Bible contains scientific truths that cause us to research and investigate because they may not be readily noticeable. Take, for example, the scripture in *Job 36:27-28: For He draws up drops of water, they distill rain from the midst, which the clouds pour down, and they drip upon man abundantly.* This reads very poetic, but as we begin to break it down, we find that Job is describing the hydrologic cycle on the earth. There is evaporation (*draws up drops of water)* from the oceans and inland waters, a transpiration (*distilled rain)* of water from plants to the clouds, and atmospheric water transport and this creates rainfall (*clouds pour down).*

The mighty Mississippi River dumps six million gallons of water per second into the Gulf of Mexico and coastal areas, but thanks to God's hydrologic cycle, we are not flooded. Scientists say that before and after Noah's flood, God stabilized the waters at a certain level upon the earth. So God, in His love for us, set the levels of the water to meet our needs. If the waters of the seas had been three meters deeper, this would have caused absorption of all the carbon dioxide and nitrogen needed to sustain life on earth, and earth would be shaped like the surface of the moon.

To further continue illustrating what I am trying to convey, I will use another example of a scripture that I have read multiple times but never truly fathomed what was being illustrated. Isaiah 40 instructs that as we wait upon the Lord, we shall renew our strength, and we would mount up with wings as eagles. I always

If GOD doesn't build the house, the builders only build shacks. Psalms 127:1 (Message)

understood the part of being patient and waiting on the Lord, and that as we wait on Him, He will renew our strength. In casual reading, I could never understand what that scripture was saying in reference to mounting up with wings of eagles. As I began to study the characteristics of an eagle, I realized that the eagle has to wait and remain perched until "thermal winds" come. In a very elementary explanation, it is the force of a draft of cool air that is forced upward from a warmer thermal wind that raises it to a higher level.

Eagles understand that this concept actually allows them to soar while seldom flapping their wings. They renew their strength by using the God-given characteristics of aerodynamics. They wait until this phenomena occurs and then they soar, allowing the Creator to lift them higher and higher while simultaneously renewing their strength. The eagle understands that it is his dependence on God's work, not its own.

With these two examples, I am not suggesting that we should become scientologists, but simply that we should dig deeper into the Word of God and allow the Holy Spirit to reveal truths as He speaks to us. The purpose of this book is not to represent a design manual or a guideline for construction. My intent is not to instruct in engineering or construction principles, but to make analogies and share fascinating angles of Bible truths that have enlightened me. I am simply trying to bridge basic principles of engineering and construction with the Kingdom of God, like Jesus did when He spoke in parables. I will make every effort to keep it light and not get into any deep engineering principles.

I set out to demonstrate the relevance of God's Word from the perspective of the reader rather than the writer. With that in

If GOD doesn't build the house, the builders only build shacks. Psalms 127:1 (Message)

mind, please note that the stories, analogies, and examples will alternate back and forth from the physical form, to the spiritual form, to an engineering form and back to the physical form, but not necessarily in that order. As a student of the scriptures, one can get lost in exegesis and theology: for instance, studying the scientific feasibility of Elijah being tele-transported in a whirlwind from heaven. The people I want to communicate with live in a world of mortgages, car payments, careers, family, and...real life. Trying to explain how Noah built such a large ark with just a few people and managed the survival of all the animals is like trying to explain the theory of relativity to a non-science person.

Early in my Christian walk, I read an engineering book called Dispensational Truth written by a mechanical engineer, Clarence Larkin. It brought the Bible alive from a mechanical engineering perspective by being full of flow charts, thermal dynamic graphs, timeline graphs and a lot of relevant pictures. This book so captivated my attention that, to this day, I can still see in my mind some of the images he portrayed in his book. For many years now, I have wanted to share the same analogies of God's Word but with a civil engineering and construction viewpoint.

I am trusting that this book will paint a picture in your mind that will stay with you for a long while. I believe that the Lord has inspired me to put these thoughts down on paper. I want to start out with a funny excerpt from a story that will depict what seems to be a reality in today's design, permitting, and construction process.

---

If God doesn't build the house, the builders only build shacks. Psalms 127:1 (Message)

# Noah Highlighting the Plans given to him By the Lord

If GOD doesn't build the house, the builders only build shacks. Psalms 127:1 (Message)

# What if Noah Tried to Build the Ark Today?

.....And the Lord spoke to Noah and said:

"In one year, I am going to make it rain and cover the whole earth with water until all flesh is destroyed, but I want you to save the righteous people and two of every kind of living thing on earth. Therefore, I am commanding you to build an Ark."

In a flash of lightning God delivered the specifications for an Ark. In fear and trembling, Noah took the plans and agreed to build the ark.

Remember," said the Lord: "You must complete the Ark and bring everything aboard in one year."

Exactly one year later, fierce storm clouds covered the earth and all the seas of the earth went into a tumult. The Lord saw that Noah was sitting in his front yard weeping.

"Noah," he shouted..."Where is the Ark?"

If GOD doesn't build the house, the builders only build shacks. Psalms 127:1 (Message)

"Lord, please forgive me," cried Noah. "I did my best, but there were big problems: First, I had to get a permit for construction, and your plans did not meet the building codes. I had to hire an engineering firm to redraw the plans."

"Then I got into a fight with the Fire Marshall and OSHA over whether or not the Ark needed a sprinkler system and approved floatation devices. Then, my neighbor objected, claiming I was violating zoning ordinances by building the Ark in my front yard, so I had to get a variance from the local planning commission. Then, I had problems getting enough wood for the Ark because there was a ban on cutting trees to protect the Spotted Owl...but, I finally convinced the U. S. Forest Service that I really needed the wood to save the owls. However, the Fish and Wildlife Service won't let me catch any owls, so, no owls."

"Then the carpenters formed a union and went on strike. I had to negotiate a settlement with the National Labor Relations Board before anyone would pick up a saw or hammer. Now, I have 16 carpenters on the Ark, but still no owls. When I started rounding up the other animals, an animal rights group sued me. They objected to me taking only two of each kind aboard mumbling something about "fairness"".

"Just when I finally got the suit dismissed, the EPA notified me that I could not complete the Ark without filing an environmental impact statement on your proposed flood. They did not take very kindly to the idea that they had no jurisdiction over the conduct of the Creator of the Universe. Then, the Army Corps of Engineers demanded a map of the proposed new flood plain. So I sent them a globe."

"Right now, I am trying to resolve a complaint filed with the Equal Employment Opportunity Commission that I am practicing discrimination by not taking Godless, unbelieving people aboard. The IRS has seized my assets, claiming that I am building the Ark in preparation to flee the country and not pay taxes. I then got a notice from a state revenue agent that I owe them some kind of user tax because I failed to register the Ark as a "recreational water craft." And finally, the ACLU got the courts to issue an injunction against further construction of

If GOD doesn't build the house, the builders only build shacks. Psalms 127:1 (Message)

the Ark, saying that since God is flooding the earth, it's a religious event, and, therefore, "unconstitutional". I really don't think I can finish the Ark for at least...another five or six years."

Noah then waited for a response from the Lord...

The sky began to clear, the sun began to shine, and the seas began to calm. A rainbow arched across the sky. Noah looked up hopefully.

"You mean you're not going to destroy the earth, Lord?"

"No," He said sadly." " I do not have to. The government already has."

If God doesn't build the house, the builders only build shacks. Psalms 127:1 (Message)

~ Page 10 ~

# The Seesaw of Our Lives

Life Pushing
Us Down

God Lifting
Us Up

If GOD doesn't build the house, the builders only build shacks. Psalms 127:1 (Message)

# Introduction

*Psalm 127:1 "Except the Lord builds a house, they labor in vain who build it..."*

$\mathcal{J}$esus is the establishment whereupon we build an existence, a vocation, a business, a congregation of disciples and our home. Too often, we endeavor to solve problems within our own knowledge and understanding, only to realize that ultimately we will fail in the process.

So many times, I have purchased an item, looked at the picture on the front of the box and thought, it is simple, I do not need instructions...***I've got this***. So before I start putting it together, I look in my toolbox, grab all the tools that I think I need, and then I am ready...***I've got this***. I disperse all the parts all over the living room. As I am assembling it, I presumed the designer messed up because he should have specified a Phillips Head screwdriver like the one I have in my hand instead of a flat head screwdriver. The reality is he provided instructions in the box I neglected to follow. I go back into my toolbox and get the correct type of screwdriver as per the directions provided in the box. Now I head back into the living room with the proper tool that the designer called for and ready to assemble it. I am so ready! Once again, I take a look at the picture on the container and persuade myself that I am so good that I do not need to bother with directions. I start assembling it on the newly carpeted floor and realize that I have to apply a lubricant to some of the mechanical parts..., but ***I've got this***. Now, I either have to move all the parts

If G O D doesn't build the house, the builders only build shacks. Psalms 127:1 (Message)

~ Page 12 ~

to a different place in the house, or else cover the carpet with some type of plastic.

To make a long story short, in the end, I have left over parts, a new carpet with grease spots all over it, and my wife is on her way home. Frustration sets in; I have parts that do not seem to coordinate; and the assembly of the object is not anything like the picture shows. Now I have to start all over.

Without fail, I blame the designer for the senseless design. I am sure that if I had designed it, it would be much easier to build and anyone could assemble it with just the picture. My advertising jargon would be **"no instructions necessary...just follow the picture."** Finally, I decide to give in and read the directions, follow the instructions, and use the right tools. In a matter of minutes, I was able to complete the task and it actually looked exactly like the picture. But I still needed to come up with an excuse for the stains on the carpet...hmm.

It is usually after a failure that you will hear, "When all else fails, follow the directions." It seems we are so full of ourselves that there is no benefit in soliciting outside help. **We got this**. We tend to rely on our own understanding and resources. We are simply too proud to ask others for assistance. We become a hindrance and make mistakes as we choose the wrong path and fail to follow the directions. In the old days before there was MapQuest and Google Earth on the phone and GPS in all the cars, some of us failed to follow the route that had been set out for us via the road maps. After all, men are born with a natural internal compass within us, and in our stubbornness we are too proud to ask anyone for directions. I have a conspiracy theory that the paper and electronic mapping companies are in cahoots with the oil companies. They give us the longest route, and concealed

If GOD doesn't build the house, the builders only build shacks. Psalms 127:1 (Message)

loops to make us use more gasoline. But actually, the bottom line is that the instructional map in the smart phone or our GPS is a tremendous help to keep us from wandering in the wilderness.

*In Isaiah 58:2-5 [2] For day after day they seek me out; they seem eager to know my ways, as if they were a nation that does what is right and has not forsaken the commands of its God. They ask me for just decisions and seem eager for God to come near them.[3] 'Why have we fasted,' they say, 'and you have not seen it? Why have we humbled ourselves, and you have not noticed? Yet on the day of your fasting, you do as you please and exploit all your workers. [4] Your fasting ends in quarreling and strife, and in striking each other with wicked fists. You cannot fast as you do today and expect your voice to be heard on high. [5] Is this the kind of fast I have chosen, only a day for people to humble themselves? Is it only for bowing one's head like a reed and for lying in sackcloth and ashes? Is that what you call a fast, a day acceptable to the LORD?*

Isaiah was speaking to people who were not following directions. Their religion had failed to live up to the high calling of service, ministry, and love. They were eager to hear the instructions of the laws but practice their own religion; they would hear one thing and do another. It seemed that they fasted so that they could get the acknowledgement of others. They prayed and gave offerings so that they could be exalted for their self-manifested conceited actions. The people of Israel included the ritual of fasting as a symbol of their goodness, yet while in the act of fasting, they were fighting and striking each other with wicked fists.

If GOD doesn't build the house, the builders only build shacks. Psalms 127:1 (Message)

They were not following the instruction manual provided to them but were demonstrating their evil practices. The outward symbols of wearing sackcloth and hurling ashes on the body, symbol of repentance, did not produce any significant changes in their lifestyle. The Word tells us that the Kingdom of God is not meat and drink, a bunch of religious rituals, but it is the right standing, peace, and joy that need to be produced. If we do not follow the Bible, our written instruction manual, we can mess up our lives, our marriages, our relationships with our children, and our relationships with the church family. Worst of all, we can mess up our relationship with God.

Many have done just that. We chose not to follow the instruction manual. The question to be asked is, "Whom can we blame for our stubbornness and rebellion?" The answer is really no one but ourselves. We are given instructions and direction, and God has gone as far as providing us the Holy Spirit that would speak into our hearts, but we have a tendency of tuning Him out. We lose the ability to hear from God and be led by Him; after all **"We got this."**

To build a building, a contractor has to follow the instructions from an architect and an engineer. The designers have deep insight on the outcome of the final product. The contractor only sees what has been laid out on the instruction manual and plans before him. He does not see the ultimate creation until the very end when it is all assembled. We do not have a complete understanding of the final outcome of our lives. If we did, it would make us a god unto ourselves. We cannot make it better; there would be parts left over. You cannot substitute something foreign. We cannot just look at a picture of someone else's life and follow it. Why? Because it is not by sight!

If God doesn't build the house, the builders only build shacks. Psalms 127:1 (Message)

God is the only one who sees and fully understands the picture in the front of the packaging. We have to take an active part, though, and actually read His plan, His specifications, and His purpose. It is not by mind. We are not smart enough to plan out and draw out a direction for our lives. I have done it so many times on my own, and the final result is that it brings me back to where I started. It is by His Spirit! God made us unique and provided us with an instructional manual (THE BIBLE) to follow and a Holy Spirit to guide us. All we have to do is read it and allow the Spirit to lead us in finishing the assembling.

Envision the imagery of building a house or a building; let us look at the vital aspects and processes that are needed to accomplish this task. In the following chapters, we will start from the point of the inception of an idea, to the point of completion and habitation, and finally, the close out.

If God doesn't build the house, the builders only build shacks. Psalms 127:1 (Message)

~ Page 16 ~

# *Sample Bar Graph of Self Evaluation*

If GOD doesn't build the house, the builders only build shacks. Psalms 127:1 (Message)

CHAPTER 1

# *Feasibility Studies*

*Proverbs 15:22 without counsel, plans go awry: but in the multitude of counselors they are established.*

*Luke 14:28-29 [28] For which of you, intending to build a tower, does not sit down first and count the cost, whether he has enough to finish it— [29] lest, after he has laid the foundation, and is not able to finish, all who see it begin to mock him.*

$\mathcal{B}$efore a construction project begins, we have to consider, study and analyze the practicality of the conceptual plan to be achieved. The feasibility study is a resource that assists the designers and provides the pertinent information that is essential to answering the vital question of "is there merit to proceeding with the proposed conceptual idea?" All activities of the investigation are focused on answering this question.

Feasibility studies have many purposes: they can be used strictly for finances and building design (as with a construction

If GOD doesn't build the house, the builders only build shacks. Psalms 127:1 (Message)

project), or they can provide information with specific data regarding the proposed property. Determining early on that a proposed building project will not work saves a lot of time, money, and heartache. Land can be like an apple...you do not know it is rotten until you take a bite. Preliminary feasibility soils studies can alert the client of possible substandard subsoil requiring the need for a unique foundation such as deep piles (large poles that are driven into the ground) to support the proposed structure, or can perhaps reveal the need for undercutting (removing bad material below the surface), bridging over, and stabilizing the subsoil; all of which are very expensive.

The study could reveal that what appears to be a green vegetative area with the potential of housing a pond could actually turn out to be an unfeasible wetland area where the federal government will not allow any land disturbance. The feasibility study can alert you to the requirements of the local municipality regarding a large detention pond to control the storm water runoff leaving from the developing site for the protection of the properties downstream. It can highlight that, if a septic system is necessary due to the lack of a public gravity line, a designated unbuildable area of the property will be required to house the septic system, and often times more property will need to be purchased.

The Highway Department may dictate that the property only be accessed from one point, or that the entrance to the property can only be a right in, and right out with no left turns. In many cases, if you are within the city limits, the city may require that the entire building to be equipped with a fire sprinkler system. All these issues can suddenly rise up and show to be very

If GOD doesn't build the house, the builders only build shacks. Psalms 127:1 (Message)

~ Page 19 ~

expensive, and the best sure way to avoid these surprises is to identify them prior to commencing construction. You can now see how this endeavor is beginning to simulate what it could be like to build Noah's Ark today.

When the builder obtains the construction plans that have been prepared by the architects and engineers and approved by the municipalities, he is not concerned if the zoning for the proposed structure meets code. He is not worried whether the footing sizes (foundation) are correct for the type of soil encountered. He simply, by faith, takes what other professionals spent time studying, calculating, evaluating, (and all those great words that end with "ing") and he acts upon it. The feasibility study will answer a lot of the questions the professionals need to complete their part and will expedite the initial process of design.

The feasibility study helps to establish and or negate specific design scenarios so they can be further studied in-depth or eliminated. As in Luke 14, it is the time to sit down and count the cost. This is the exploratory expedition of the pre-construction process where a number of alternatives under consideration are quickly eliminated. But the fact that the initial investigation is negative does not mean that the proposal does not have merit. Sometimes limitations or inadequacies found due to the feasibility study can be eliminated with resourceful engineering. The project designers need to examine the feasibility study and challenge its

If GOD doesn't build the house, the builders only build shacks. Psalms 127:1 (Message)

underlying assumptions. As they accumulate information and investigate alternatives, either a positive or a negative outcome may emerge. Major stumbling blocks may materialize that negate the project.

It is at this point that the content of the feasibility study is weighed against the purpose of the project. Sometimes we have these challenges in our lives and realize they can be overcome because, with God, all things are possible. The go/no-go decision leads to a point of no return...the point where total trust in God is required. With a construction project, that point would be where finances are in order, materials are available, the labor force is ready, and work begins. The feasibility study provides necessary information for decision-making. It gives focus to the project and narrows down the alternatives. It enriches the probability of success by addressing mitigating factors early on that could affect the project. It can help in securing funding from lending institutions and other monetary sources to prove the viability of the project. The feasibility study is a critical step in the assessment process.

I speak from experience that commencing a construction project after having a favorable feasibility study is a simple thing to do. But finishing it without all the resources is one of the most stressful endeavors to undertake. Jesus teaches that discipleship must include planning and sacrifice. He instructs that, before a person begins to build, he should be sure he is willing and able to pay the full cost of the project. This includes time, money, and physical stamina. Christian living is costly living; we must count on forsaking the snares of this world; we must be willing to run the full distance to arrive at the Kingdom of God; we must be willing

If GOD doesn't build the house, the builders only build shacks. Psalms 127:1 (Message)

to pay the full price of discipleship. If we do not itemize the cost necessary prior to establishing and laying the foundation, it can lead to a humiliating and disgraceful failure. Nevertheless, an unfinished life is far more catastrophic than a failed foundation. Jesus warns in *Luke 9:62 ..."No one, having put his hand to the plow, and looking back, is fit for the Kingdom of God."* Failure to count the cost of following Christ results in an incomplete and devastated life.

I have been a Christian for over 38 years and at the beginning, there were people who thought it was a whim I was going through and it would pass. Their viewpoint was that I was not considering the cost. There were times when I was ridiculed for the new person I had become. There were trials and temptations and moments of wanting to concede. But I am proud that I serve a King who has walked with me and at times has carried me and has replaced all the hurt feelings of my past life with His love and acceptance. It is with His help alone that I have been able to remain faithful. I am still under construction and, in some cases, being remodeled. The project is not finished, the calling has never left, and He is still working on me.

*Philippians 1:6 being confident of this, He who began a good work in me will carry it on to completion until the day of Christ Jesus.*

Of this, I am thankful every day. On the other hand, there are other times in our lives when God commands us to do something that needs to be fulfilled in faith; no questions asked, no feasibility studies. As the Nike slogan says, "Just do it."

If GOD doesn't build the house, the builders only build shacks. Psalms 127:1 (Message)

Abraham was a man of faith, a man who obeyed when he was asked by the Lord to sacrifice the promised son, Isaac. But you know the rest of the story; God in His ultimate mercy provided the substitute Lamb.

When God asked Moses to lead the Children of Israel out of Egypt, God was very clear He was going before them to prepare the way.

*Exodus 23:20 "Behold, I send an Angel before you to keep you in the way and to bring you into the place which I have prepared."*

At the burning bush, God told Moses what the land was like. The Land of Canaan was a good and large land; a land flowing with milk and honey. God knew there were giants in the land and He was not caught by surprise.

He went as far as instructing Moses that He would send His angel to drive out the enemies (giants) ahead of them. When we act on our own, we become a singularity, and taking action without any direction from the Lord is a lonely place to be when things do not go as we had planned them to go. The good news is that He is a merciful and a loving God in spite of our rebellious ways.

If GOD doesn't build the house, the builders only build shacks. Psalms 127:1 (Message)

*Numbers 13:1 And the LORD spoke to Moses, saying, "Send men to spy out the land of Canaan, which I am giving to*

*the children of Israel; from each tribe of their fathers you shall send a man, everyone a leader among them." So Moses sent them from the Wilderness of Paran according to the command of the LORD, all of them men who were heads of the children of Israel.*

Often in our Christian walk, God gives us a command and instead of acting on it, we have a tendency to evaluate, calculate, analyze, and reason with the "feasibility" of what God has charged us with. Deuteronomy 1:20-25 reveals how the plan to send spies did not directly originate with Moses, but instead came from the people. You see, the Children of Israel showed little faith in God; they had to work it out themselves; they had to see the promise. Verse 22 "...Let us send men ahead to spy out the land for us and bring back a report about the route we are to take and the towns we will come to."

Moses instructed them that they were to go take the land as God had commanded, but the people suggested a different plan. He went along with it, and these instructions to the spies were a direct manifestation of unbelief. It was not the original instruction from God to send spies, but He allowed it.

God commands Moses to send men out to the Land of Canaan, the land of promise, the land flowing with milk and honey. At that point, the people seemed to sense they were more on a mission from themselves than on a mission from God.

If GOD doesn't build the house, the builders only build shacks. Psalms 127:1 (Message)

The spies believed they were on a reconnaissance mission to prepare a necessary feasibility study. The spying and reporting was not for God to receive information, or for Him to consider the feasibility of occupying this land. God knew all of the information ahead of time. What God had promised about the land was true and did not need any additional investigating. The spies who explored Canaan should have outlined in depth the reality, strengths and weaknesses of all they saw. From the story in Numbers 13, all of the twelve spies agreed on what they saw: land flowing with milk and honey, large fruit, strong men, fortified cities, and giants. From their feasibility study, they were able to see the pros and cons of their "project." Thankfully, two of the twelve spies also "saw" and still believed the command given to Moses by God through the burning bush. The other ten failed to recognize God already had the plan in place for each "con" they encountered.

There are so many times that God will allow us to figure things out for ourselves and most of the time, the result is catastrophic. This expedition had an unfortunate result; but nevertheless, it fit into the plan of God. He used the report of the spies as a test of Israel's faith.

If GOD doesn't build the house, the builders only build shacks. Psalms 127:1 (Message)

Chapter 2

*The Blueprints*

*1 Chronicles 28:11-12 - Then David gave to his son Solomon the plans for the vestibule, its houses, its treasuries, its upper chamber, its inner chambers, and the place of the mercy seat, 12 and the plans for all that he had by the spirit, of the courts of the house of the Lord, of all the chambers all around...*

We have to imagine that this was a large set of detailed

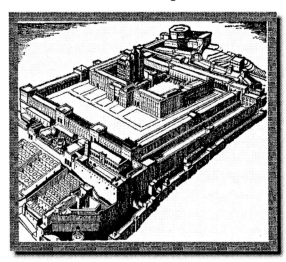

construction plans that David gave Solomon for him to build all these structures. Let us evaluate the plans that it would take to build a single house for us. We will start out by assuming that we have no knowledge about the process of building. The only thing that we are certain about is that we need building materials, (cement, lumber, nails, plumbing, electrical, roofing materials, etc.). We go

If GOD doesn't build the house, the builders only build shacks. Psalms 127:1 (Message)

to the nearest lumberyard, purchase what we think is needed for the construction, and we have the materials delivered to the property and place them in a designated staging area. We start sawing and nailing boards together. We pull electrical wires through the walls and set pipes for the plumbing in some assumed location. When we are finished, we come to the realization that all the effort expended without the benefit of a set of plans yielded a result that does not look like the picture we are modeling the house after. What we need is a plan, a drawing, and a blueprint.

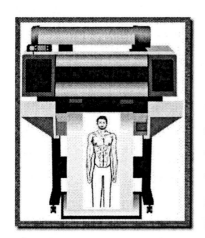

In order to build a house, a sets of blueprints is essential because it shows the design, measurements, specifications, and materials necessary to build the structure. No one in his right mind would consider building a house without the information that a professional has etched on a blueprint. Yet while we would not think of building a house without a blueprint, many of us go about building our lives and our families with no idea of God's plan for our lives. We have a blueprint that was bought and paid for and freely given to us by the shed blood of the Architect of our lives. Yet we do not seek instruction and counsel from the Architect, and all too often, the end result is a decrepit family life. The Designer, God, has taken the time to prepare a set of blueprints that resemble what He proposed the house would look like. He

If GOD doesn't build the house, the builders only build shacks. Psalms 127:1 (Message)

detailed it in His Word, activated it with His Son, and sent the Project Manager (The Holy Spirit) to assure that the specifications are followed according to His plans.

The blueprints are not corruptible or perishable. Once the set of plans comes out of the printer, it is not to be changed. It is the portrayal of what the Chief Architect inspired it to be...a perfect design with no errors or omissions. If we want it to look different, it is no longer the original plan. It becomes a modified version of the original. Unfortunately, sometimes during the construction of a house, we choose to make changes in the field in order to aim for a different finished product. We make these changes without any consideration that the designer did not intend for that change to happen. Too often, our revisions influence other members of the structure in a negative way. For instance, a wall cannot haphazardly be removed without proving it is not a load-bearing (support) wall. Once revisions are made, the original is no longer the original but a modified version. The only person that can alter the original drawing is the designer. He is the only one that knows exactly what impact one change can make on the rest of the house. When a person becomes a Christian, revisions are made on the original blueprints by the Architect Himself.

2 Corinthians 5:17 explains that God permanently erased the old sins from the original blueprint and added a new design to bring the plan into compliance according to the building code (The Word). The blueprints are precious and significant to our lives. They are not useless marks thrown on a paper to produce a drawing. They have meaning; they represent interpretation; they

If GOD doesn't build the house, the builders only build shacks. Psalms 127:1 (Message)

~ Page 28 ~

give instruction; they project an image that will only be seen when the builder follows it through to the last detail.

The Chief Architect knows every line, every dot, and every mark placed on the original drawing. He is so involved in the design that He knows each and every part and inscription on the plans. He is so detailed that the plans include an individualized copyright on the thumb of each design that no other plan has the same inscription. He knows exactly how many hairs are on our heads at all times.

As an engineer, I come up with alternative solutions to a design; Alternative "A," Alternative "B," etc. I try to find ways to build it cheaper, called value engineering. I may, at times, make errors and omissions and try to correct them. However, with God, there are no alternatives. It was His intention to only have one design, one original, and one blueprint. God did not make a mistake when He created us. He does not have an eraser or a backspace button on a computer to correct an error He made. He made us perfect, but in our rebellion, we choose to alter the original design.

John 3:16 tells us that He loved us enough in our wayward state that He was willing to offer His only son to bring us back into compliance with the original plan. Jesus became the **"control-alt-delete"** to give us a fresh boot up, a new start.

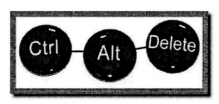

If GOD doesn't build the house, the builders only build shacks. Psalms 127:1 (Message)

*Jeremiah 29: 11 for I know the plans I have for you, declares the Lord, plans to prosper you, and not to harm you, plans to give you hope and a future. (NIV)*

The blueprints were laid out long before the foundation of the world. He had me on the drawing board designing me uniquely, pouring Himself into me. His very hands and thoughts had an active part in what I would look like, how I would talk, who I would become. I was not an accident that caught Him by surprise, but a manifestation and an expression of Himself. I am a child of God. I have His character. His love and affection is toward

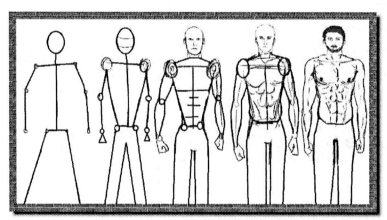

me. Yet, with the rest of creation, He simply spoke and it obeyed.

With me, He drew every line on the paper, every curve, every circle, and every geometric figure my human body could possibly possess. On the drawing board, I may have started as a stick figure but when He was through, He looked at me, smiled, and was pleased, for I was a mirror image of Him. I am not an accident. God used a thought process beyond our comprehension. After the drawings were completed, then He

If GOD doesn't build the house, the builders only build shacks. Psalms 127:1 (Message)

molded me, shaped me, breathed into me, and gave me life. I am precious in His sight and wonderfully made. The scripture in Jeremiah 29 says, "*I know the plans I have.*" Only God knows the plans for our lives. He knows the beginning, the middle, and the end.

Buildings, like humans, are not carelessly thrown together. A lot of planning takes place long before the first patch of dirt is turned over. As mentioned earlier, a set of plans (blueprints) are drawn up so that the builder knows exactly how to put the building together. This can be a layer of many plans with many disciplines. The main concept here is that only the architect or designer knows the final outcome and only he can see through all the details on each plan. There are numerous pages of plans that are drawn by the designer to convey the process for the construction of a structure. Many disciplines are involved in preparing the plans, such as geotechnical, civil, structural, mechanical, and electrical.

There are so many plans that, at times, one discipline may not be aware of what the other discipline is doing. For example, the HVAC engineer (heating, ventilating, and air conditioning) may not necessarily know what the

If GOD doesn't build the house, the builders only build shacks. Psalms 127:1 (Message)

foundation engineering plans are depicting and specifying, yet both are equally important in the completion of the project. This is why it is so important for each discipline to communicate with each other in unison and to harmoniously fulfill the original design.

There are layers, upon layers, upon layers, upon layers of plans with detailed importance. We have a tendency to discard any plans we believe are not significant to our lives. There are so many times in my life when I am facing what may be a trial or difficulty. I start wondering what that specific plan is for. What value does it have? Why am I facing such a trial? I do not understand this particular plan, and how it fits in the larger scheme of all the plans that He has for me. Often times, I am not able to see the benefit of what has been laid out on this particular sheet of the stack of plans. Frankly, like the contractor, I do not understand, until I go to the next sheet of the plans, and then I can look back and realize the benefit.

*1 Corinthians 13:11 when I was a child, I spoke as a child, I understood as a child, thought as a child: but when I became a man, I put away childish things.*

When we are young, we rely on those who provide for us. We have no thought as to what our profession is going to be, or where the money will come from to pay the mortgage. We do not concern ourselves about such things, and we do not plan ahead. We are usually living for that day with no care in the world. Nevertheless, we also want to do the things that grownups do.

If GOD doesn't build the house, the builders only build shacks. Psalms 127:1 (Message)

We want to drive, stay up late, and have spending money in our pockets. As we get older, we look back and realize what God was doing in our lives during the journey. The problem we have is that, when we are young, we want to skip the crucial elementary parts of the process.

The completed designed structure is only achieved by following the original plans. For example, a significant step in construction is the placing of the floor joist. This is an unseen member of the flooring system that gets covered up and will only be noticed if failure occurs. To save money and time, some contractors may cut corners and exclude the required number and spacing of nails required to properly fasten the joists.

It is certain that the floor system will fail without following what the designer called for, even if it seems to be insignificant or unseen. Likewise, in our own lives, we will fail if we do not follow through with the things we may assume are insignificant and unseen.

There is an outlined procedure in the construction process that we have to follow. We must learn to crawl before we can walk, and learn to walk before we can run, and we can be assured that the Designer takes pleasure in watching us develop, just as we do with our own children. We may think it is irrelevant and a waste of time, but the process builds character. It would be shocking if one day you went by a construction site and the next day a 10-story building appeared on it. It would perplex our minds; we are not capable of handling such an event.

We realize many factors determine the length of time for construction, such as complexity of design, financing, permitting,

If GOD doesn't build the house, the builders only build shacks. Psalms 127:1 (Message)

~ Page 33 ~

site preparation, availability of materials and laborers, and a key factor, weather. For a typical 10-story building, a minimum of 24 months of construction would be a good estimate for completion. Likewise, we do not expect a newborn baby to suddenly start walking and talking in the delivery room. There is a process. There is a course. There are learning times. There are growing times, and there are things we do not comprehend that must take place in our lives. The plans are too intricate for our minute minds, but God sees the final product and knows that the development of our spirit, soul, and body must follow His plan.

Our lives start at the beginning, listening, learning, and getting direction from the Lord to grow and implement His plan. Similarly, the construction process begins with the feasibility study, blueprints, actual building, and finally results in a structure. During the journey of the "process," there are times we are not sure of the plans He has for us and we may take steps into uncharted territory.

In the fall of 2005, I went through a process of grasping the promise of Jeremiah 29:11 in a very personal way. God told us He *"plans to prosper you and not to harm you, plans to give you hope and a future."* I set out to do something that I felt, in my heart, was directed by the Lord At the time, we lived in Atlanta and owned an engineering and surveying company, but for some reason, I felt impressed to move to Alabama and develop a residential subdivision.

"My plan" was to go there and build houses with bricks and sticks. "God's plan" was for me to build relationships with love, care, and concern. Being an engineer and a builder, I only saw a

If GOD doesn't build the house, the builders only build shacks. Psalms 127:1 (Message)

~ Page 34 ~

large subdivision with many houses and amenities in it. I had every street laid out in my mind, and chose the corresponding names specifically to glorify God and to serve as a witnessing tool. I knew where every property corner was to be placed, the number on each lot, the location of the sanitary sewer and water line, and how the storm water was to be controlled.

During a meeting with the city planning commission, a question arose regarding the origin of the street names. This allowed me the opportunity to share the Gospel with the members without them realizing what was coming. The street names God impressed upon me were: Aventura, Destino,

Esperansa, Gloria, and Carino. I was given the liberty, and I shared with them each meaning. First, Aventura is the *adventure* that becomes a wonderful life when we walk with Jesus. Then I continued to share with the commission that we have Destino, our *destiny* to share Esperansa, which is the *hope* of Gloria, His *glory*, with others. It is through our testimony we express Carino,

If GOD doesn't build the house, the builders only build shacks. Psalms 127:1 (Message)

the ultimate *love* of God, and the Gospel will be revealed through a practical application. Time and time again, I would use this witnessing tool to show Jesus to people.

**"For I knew the plans I had for it."**

However in my pride and arrogance, I set out to do things with my own understanding and with my own capabilities. Now, I can look back and see the places and times where the Lord was there to fulfill His promise to keep me from harm and to accomplish His purpose.

I was alone at the site demolishing an old house and cleaning around several large pecan trees with a bulldozer. The bulldozer was equipped with a cage and shield in the front to protect the operator from any foreign objects. In my lack of wisdom, I raised the shield so that it would not obstruct my vision. I did not notice, however, that one of the large branches of the tree was caught on the bulldozer and as I was looking down at the ground I was clearing, the branch snapped into the cab and slapped me in the forehead, causing me to lose consciousness. When I came to, I found myself at the other end of the property at the bottom of a roadside ditch. Miraculously, He kept me from harm as He promised. To be honest with you, I enjoyed driving that tractor so much that I got back on it many more times, but I learned a valuable lesson, and that is to follow the instructions of keeping the shield down.

As construction sites can be hazardous, I believe there are numerous times I was protected from harm. A different time, I was supervising a crew hanging siding on an unusual peak of a house. Watching them frustrated me because they were not

If GOD doesn't build the house, the builders only build shacks. Psalms 127:1 (Message)

~ Page 36 ~

installing it as I designed it. I told them to get down and let me do it correctly! Without taking necessary safety measures, I quickly climbed to the top of the 20-foot ladder. Because of my hurriedness and lack of patience, I did not take the time to secure the ladder. I fell to the ground and shattered my heel. From such a height and with all the construction debris that was lying where I fell, it was a miracle that only my heel was broken. Again, He promised, "*not to harm me.*"

If I had followed the instructions as dictated in the OSHA (Occupational Safety and Health Administration) Manual, I would not have suffered for six weeks and caused a delay in the construction of that house. Despite my carelessness and rebellion, the Lord has kept me and protected me from so many disasters in my life.

*Jeremiah 29: 11 for I know the plans I have for you, declares the Lord, plans to prosper you, and not to harm you, plans to give you hope and a future. (NIV)*

Jeremiah gave this prophesy to the Children of Israel while they were experiencing great pain. Even though it would be another 70 years before this prophecy would be fulfilled, God wanted them to know they were in His plan. He is interested in His children's welfare.

A question arises though: What is meant by prosper? And what is prosperity? It does not necessarily mean we are going to be wealthy with the material riches of this world. There is nothing wrong with material wealth in itself, especially when surrounded

---

If GOD doesn't build the house, the builders only build shacks. Psalms 127:1 (Message)

by a generous heart. That scripture catches our attention and we tune in because we think God is going to give us money. The Word could have been very specific in this prophecy if money was the object. The fact of the matter is that God is not speaking primarily about money. He wants us to prosper, emotionally, physically and spiritually, so that we are being fulfilled. We are thriving, flourishing, and enjoying His blessings in every area of our lives.

A contractor can cut corners and use smaller wood than the plans call for, thus making the structure weaker than the designer intended for it to be. Once they are covered with plywood, those studs are no longer seen, but with time, the structure will show signs of weakness, stress, and possibly buckling. The contractor may have saved some money and increased his profit margin. He may have covered up the sin (smaller wood, fewer nails) but the shortcut will eventually show up. Sooner or later we have to pay.

God knows every stud and nail that is supposed to go into the structure. He will not be mocked, and we cannot hide anything from Him. Integrity goes hand-in-hand with prosperity, even if it causes us to lose money. For us to be prospered by the Lord, we have to do what is right in His eyes. He always provides us an opportunity to make right what is wrong. As we confess or disclose any error or omission in the building process, it will be much easier to correct it before it gets covered up. By taking care of the error or omission, we can prevent costly repairs and embarrassment.

If GOD doesn't build the house, the builders only build shacks. Psalms 127:1 (Message)

Proverbs 28:13 says it clearly: *He who covers his sins will not prosper, but whoever confesses and forsakes them shall have mercy.*

His plans in my life have been many, and to some degree, too complicated for me to understand. God is not interested in a Lone Ranger who is going to do things his way without any care as to what God's will is. He does not want someone that follows his own agenda, designs his own future, and neglects God's plan for his life. I am always reminded of the scripture *Mark 8:36: "For what will it profit a man if he gains the whole world and loses his own soul."* I do not understand a lot of what He does. All I know is that I have to trust in what He sets out for me and follow His plan. I question why some things happen the way they do while I am going through them. Later, though, I look back and realize His plan was to *"give me hope and a future."* Some people are mistaken in thinking that financial security is God's way of prospering them. It may be a by-product of obedience and following His commands, but it is not the ultimate sign that we have achieved how He intended to prosper us.

Visiting many undeveloped countries, I have come to realize that some of those wonderful people experience a far more prosperous life than what I have experienced. They may not have earthly riches, but they have peace and joy. Their family unit is so close-fitting that they work together and take care of each other. We worry about things that really should not matter. We stress out to the point that we need medical attention. The wealth that we work so hard to attain is spent laying down on a

If GOD doesn't build the house, the builders only build shacks. Psalms 127:1 (Message)

couch, paying another person to listen to our problems. We stay up all night thinking how to deal with the stock market when it goes down (sell, don't sell, buy, don't buy).

Jesus does not teach that if we listen and act on His teachings that He will spare us from suffering and hard times. He never promises our hearts will not be broken, that our bodies will not fail, or that grief will not bring us to our knees. Jesus does not say that the floods will not come, but instead He instructs us to build our house on Him, the rock. Then we will be able to weather whatever storm comes our way. Every day is a new day we should look forward to, a day of prospering with our families, a day of prospering with our friends.

The wisest and richest man on the earth, upon acquiring all the possessions he desired, was not satisfied. He claimed that all is vanity and there is nothing new under the sun. This man, Solomon, built a great temple with many plans prepared by engineers and architects, but he missed the key part...God was not through with Him, and there was more under the sun for him. Yes, Solomon had developed and built his dreams, but, along the way, he lost vision. God will show us His plans, not only to prosper us and give us hope and a future, but also to give us vision.

As I set out to build several subdivisions in Alabama, God blessed me with Christian partners: men of integrity, sound mind, and sound judgment who would stick it out with me until the very end. We suffered setbacks, first due to the economy and then due to the oil spill in the Gulf. *"Plans to prosper you and not to harm you, plans to give you hope and a future."* I recalled the days I spent crying out loud in the middle of the field of that large tract of land

If GOD doesn't build the house, the builders only build shacks. Psalms 127:1 (Message)

~ Page 40 ~

that was supposed to be a subdivision. I recall praying and accusing God of not keeping his promise of prospering me. *"Plans to prosper you and not to harm you, plans to give you hope and a future."* I questioned Him as a polished prosecuting attorney would question his defendant. I had questions and no responses. I felt that He was not there; that He did not like me; that He had simply abandoned me. All along, my partners believed in the Lord and in me. I remember one of the partners saying, "This is God's property." I could not see that. All I could see was the failure, the vast vacant land that was supposed to be a subdivision. *"Plans to prosper you and not to harm you, plans to give you hope and a future."*

During the process of what I was calling a failure, the Lord was prospering me in unseen ways. One such instance came when a young lady drove past our subdivision on her way to an appointment with a realtor to purchase a house in another subdivision. By divine appointment, she saw our sign, stopped, and loved our designs. She bought one of our houses that day. Little did I realize that we were helping her build a spiritual house with the Lord, not only a physical house made of bricks and sticks, but a dwelling place fill with affection and understanding. She gave her life, love, and affection to the Lord. The scripture tell us that Jesus is a friend that sticks closer than a brother. She became the epitome of that scripture and, to this day, is a very close friend and sister. I ended up in the hospital with adult onset Type 2 Diabetes and my newfound sister, Becky Kersh, along with another dear friend and doctor, Dr. Jacob Gruel, was there to nurture me through the process.

If GOD doesn't build the house, the builders only build shacks. Psalms 127:1 (Message)

Another time, a friend who was going through the same financial hardship and failure as I was came to my office in desperation. He brought a revolver with Him, and wanted to take his life. He was compelled to tell someone the reasons why he was such a failure and why he no longer was fit to live. Only the Lord could reveal to me the things I needed to share with him. I am not a trained counselor. I am not an eloquent speaker, and I had no idea from my own mind what to tell him. As we talked, the Holy Spirit allowed me to see the very things that I was going through. In the midst of my darkness, He reminded me how prosperous I was because of my great family and friends that truly care. To this day, I do not remember what I said to my friend, but he immediately went to see a pastor friend and gave his life to the Lord.

The bricks and sticks only define what I do, what I design and build, not who I am. I have a great hope and future ahead of me and want to develop it and prosper it with Jesus on my side. The fact that I come out of a trial without material wealth does not mean that I did not prosper. I would like to earn jewels for my crown in heaven as I spend the rest of my life here on earth. God designed the plans for my life and He is always there to carry me through, even when I deviate or do not understand the future for my life. *"Plans to prosper me and not to harm me, plans to give me hope and a future."*

If GOD doesn't build the house, the builders only build shacks. Psalms 127:1 (Message)

~ Page 42 ~

# Building Our Lives from the Ground Up

If GOD doesn't build the house, the builders only build shacks. Psalms 127:1 (Message)

**Chapter 3**

# *Preparing the Ground*

*Ecclesiastes 11:6 In the morning sow your seed, and in the evening do not withhold your hand; For you do not know which will prosper, either this or that, or whether both alike will be good.*

$\mathcal{J}$esus spread the good news of His love no matter how mucky, dry, rocky or weed-infested the ground was. He plowed and broke through the hard pans of our lives, tilling the ground until we were ready for seed. The ground must be prepared before seed can be planted. John the Baptist came ahead of our Lord telling people to prepare the way. Jesus already knew the place where he would sow, what fruit that it would bear, and that it would be good.

We, too, are called to sow seed to this lost world. The seeds of God's love, God's justice, God's blessing, and God's forgiveness are all precious and limitless. These seeds have been sown in us to allow us to flourish, and to make us in His likeness to be His laborers, preparing and proclaiming Him for the harvest. One of the most exciting parts of a construction project is when the heavy equipment finally arrives on the site and excavation and hauling of soil material begins.

If GOD doesn't build the house, the builders only build shacks. Psalms 127:1 (Message)

Before any of the land can be disturbed, however, a geotechnical engineer is hired to test the soil, to investigate its

soil-bearing capacity and to prepare a report with recommendations to rectify any problems encountered. The field test consists of taking soil borings (drilling a 4-inch auger) at designated places on the site, gathering soil samples, and preparing a report that indicates the depth, type and layer of soils, as well as water table, permeability, and cohesion of the soils.

The report will also show if the site was used to bury debris or if there were any alluvial materials (soft soils left by floods) encountered, both of which would require additional action before construction can begin. All this is pertinent information that the structural engineer needs to have in order to design the proper foundation.

*Luke 8:4-8, ⁴ when a great multitude had gathered, and they had come to Him from every city, He spoke by a parable:*

If GOD doesn't build the house, the builders only build shacks. Psalms 127:1 (Message)

*⁵ "A sower went out to sow his seed. And as he sowed, some fell by the wayside; and it was trampled down, and the birds of the air devoured it. ⁶ Some fell on rock; and as soon as it sprang up, it withered away because it lacked moisture. ⁷ And some fell among thorns, and the thorns sprang up with it and choked it.*

*⁸ But others fell on good ground, sprang up, and yielded a crop a hundredfold." When He had said these things He cried, "He who has ears to hear, let him hear!"*

To explain the importance of sowing, Jesus used this parable to show four different types of surfaces where seed was sowed. The first seed fell by the wayside, implying the sower was spreading seed recklessly, with no thought or plan. As a result, it was trampled  down and the birds devoured it. We cannot arbitrarily choose any place to build. We have to be sure that it would be the most suitable place to build. Reckless building without any type of preparation can cause it to fall by the wayside. We should be sure that it is He who is directing us and that we are listening and yielding ourselves to Him and His guidelines.

The second seed landed on a rock where it began to grow, but then it withered due to lack of moisture. Building on a rock

If GOD doesn't build the house, the builders only build shacks. Psalms 127:1 (Message)

has its challenges.  For instance, the footing for a new building cannot easily be dug out but may, depending on the formation of the rock, have to be blasted out with explosives.  With a specific design, however, building on rock (if not fractured) is great for the structural integrity of the home or building, although it is not suitable for landscaping due to lack of moisture and topsoil.

The third seed did fall into dirt that appeared suitable.  After the crop began to grow, another crop grew beside it.  This crop came from the seed of jealousy; the seed that comes to kill, steal and destroy.  In an effort to keep the bad seed from taking over the good seed, there has to be a removal of the bad seed.

What we have to apply is **ROUNDUP ™** to get rid of it, so that it does not take away the hope of increase.  One of the great advantages of using Roundup™ is that it penetrates down to the root of the problem that would choke our relationship with God and others.  By simply pulling it out, we may not get all of the root and some will remain that will creep up at a later time.  We have to apply a roundup of prayer, the Word, and direction from the

If GOD doesn't build the house, the builders only build shacks. Psalms 127:1 (Message)

Holy Spirit to really saturate the thing that will keep us from increase. It takes a lot of work to remove unwanted weeds that would choke out what we want to harvest. Building on unprepared soil is a formula leading to certain failure. While this parable relates to hearts receiving the Word of God, it shows the importance of suitable soil as the initial component to a successful venture.

When we begin the process of plowing the ground in preparation for a new building, there are times we will encounter large obstacles that appear to be immovable. If we are determined to build on this site, it will require considerable digging, horsepower, dedication, and commitment to move and discard the obstacles. It may take a lot of work; hard work that at times is not pleasant. We have to work the ground during the heat of the day, long hours into the evening. It can be challenging and lonely work to remove those immovable obstacles. Other times, we may need someone to come lend a hand; someone to spot for us and guide us along the way so that we stay on course. That help may come from our pastor or someone who has had experience in moving obstacles in their own lives.

Sometimes we become callused to the point that, when we receive a seed, it dies for the lack of nurturing and watering. We become hardened by unbelief. Perhaps you prayed for something and your prayer was not answered. I personally experienced this when, as mentioned earlier, I was developing a subdivision. I was tilling, plowing, and preparing the ground. Yet when an immovable obstacle was encountered, I stopped instantly, and I was ready to give up. I prayed and asked God to

If GOD doesn't build the house, the builders only build shacks. Psalms 127:1 (Message)

~ Page 48 ~

help me build this subdivision and asked Him to remove the obstacles.

I incorrectly concluded, however, that God does not answer prayers, at least not for me. Bitterness and hardness took over my heart. When I finally reached a point of surrender, I was broken before Him, and I cried out with heartfelt confession and repentance. I realized that He had been there all the time plowing deep in me, preparing the soil for His purpose, not mine. Where there seemed to be no way, He provided a way. I then allowed Him to plow and move the boulders out of the way so He could plant a new seed in my life and work His will in the subdivision.

A foundation for a structure that is placed on a piece of land filled with stumps, brush, water and rocks can be disastrous for the structure. At first, the effects may not be seen, but with time, it will manifest the weakness of the soil that was hidden underneath.

The more time spent preparing the soil for the foundation, the more likely that anything that is built on that foundation will

If GOD doesn't build the house, the builders only build shacks. Psalms 127:1 (Message)

not crumble, crack, fall, or lean. That is the reason you see tractors, bulldozers and heavy pieces of equipment spending many days clearing a site, hauling off debris, bringing in good soil, and driving back and forth to obtain a level and compacted surface. This driving back and forth is the process necessary to achieve a strong base. Optimum moisture content (watering) in the ground is also crucial for the compaction ratio to be acceptable. The contractor may have to add the precise amount of moisture needed. As a result, the compaction ratio will produce a strong base for the foundation. If alluvial soil (highly organic soil) is found, it has to removed and hauled away. Good soil is brought in and placed in layers (6 inch to 12 inches deep) and individually compacted by a heavy piece of equipment. The process will continue from the lower strata (layer) until it reaches the surface.

How does that relate to us? Visualize that once bad soil is exposed, whether through the Word or Holy Spirit, it has to be removed from our lives. Then we have the process of replacing the bad stuff with new material found in Him. New material is compacted layer upon layer, line upon line, and precept upon precept, to get us back to the good ground that God used to form us. It takes work and faith. Without all the effort, the foundation once built on this base will fail. The failure will not be seen readily, but with time, it will manifest within the structure. An analysis of the failure will prove the failure begins at the bottom of the lower strata, where little care was taken in proper compaction.

*1Timothy 5:24 - 25 24 some men's sins are clearly evident, preceding them to judgment, but those of some men follow*

If GOD doesn't build the house, the builders only build shacks. Psalms 127:1 (Message)

~ Page 50 ~

*later.* **²⁵ Likewise, the good works of some are clearly evident, and those that are otherwise cannot be hidden.**

Preparing a site for building construction can be a long process depending on the information from the geotechnical engineer. As mentioned above, optimum moisture is essential to good compaction, but what if a site has good soil with excess water? A common practice to rid the soil of the surplus water is called *consolidation*. Basically, a specified amount of soil is hauled onto the site and a mound of soil is placed where a future structure is to be constructed. The geotechnical engineer calculates the size of the mound and the length of time the mound will stay, up to a year. The weight of the mound placed on the site squeezes the soil below and removes any unwanted water that would cause weaknesses. It also brings the soil's particles below the surface closer together as it removes the unwanted water and air voids, thus tightening the soil and making it stronger.

The same process can occur when life seems to squeeze us without relief. We do not like to be pressed; we do not like to be squeezed by the burdens, cares, sicknesses, and trials that life brings upon us. Sometimes this process is necessary. This consolidation will rid our lives of unoccupied places not filled with the Holy Spirit. The most amazing thing happens when the immense mound of soil is eventually removed: We are released from our afflictions, freed from our voids, and we become stronger.

Builders must be confident that the ground has been prepared adequately before continuing the construction as per the design and as shown on the blueprints. On the surface, it may look strong and flawless, but there is nothing worse than a

If GOD doesn't build the house, the builders only build shacks. Psalms 127:1 (Message)

~ Page 51 ~

deficient surface. Tests need to be performed to verify if the type of soil encountered on the surface is the same throughout the deeper layers and is adequate for the proposed design. Soil may be sandy on the surface, but a few inches below, the soil boring may confirm that a heavy clay soil exists that has no drainage capability. Unless this finding is considered in design and construction, failure will ensue.

Only with the completion of a thorough soil investigation can the type and depth of the footing and foundation required for the building be determined. Even if the footing, slab, and its vertical components are constructed of a rigid material like concrete, as called out in the specifications, they will only be as strong as the ground they are resting on.

The Tower of Pisa is "leaning" in light of the fact that its foundation went just 3 meters deep, excessively shallow for such a structure. Additionally, it was constructed on ground that was not adequately prepared and was insecure in nature.

***2 Timothy 2:15 be diligent to present yourself approved to God, a worker who does not need to be ashamed, rightly dividing the word of truth.***

Just as the geotechnical engineer studies the soil, we too have to study to be certain that we realize not only what needs to be purged in our lives, but also what needs to be added. When we

If GOD doesn't build the house, the builders only build shacks. Psalms 127:1 (Message)

~ Page 52 ~

ask Jesus to come into our lives, we become a new creature in Christ, but we ought to continually be tilling, studying, pressing, and removing any foreign elements (habits, attitudes, and ways) to keep the ground strong and fruitful. This is where the Holy Spirit through the Word will speak to us daily, pointing out specific areas of weakness and foreign matter (junk) that need to be excavated and hauled to the landfill. We cannot be superficial, shallow Christians, lest we fall. The deeper we dig in the Word of God and allow the Holy Spirit to change us, the less likely we are to be ashamed of a failed structure.

One truth about bad soil is that damage is progressive. Similarly, in our lives, sin starts out with a little white lie, and progressively covers one lie with another. The void or unremoved imperfections start out small and worsen as the load of the foundation begins to settle.

However, the good news is that **"The Good News"** was given to us even in our failed state. God in his mercy makes provisions to restore us to a stable relationship with Him. He may provide groups of people that will help us carry the load when at times we are not able to bear it alone.

Damaging progressive subsidence or sinking in our lives will eventually lead to a failed structure. It is at this point, that God undergirds us with underpinning piles by penetrating our lives with additional support. The bad news is that if we are too stubborn, and we do not acknowledge weakness and cry out for help, then the damage will become worse. We sink deeper and deeper into trouble and it will require many more piers to underpin us. The cost is expensive, damaging, and can result in catastrophe.

If GOD doesn't build the house, the builders only build shacks. Psalms 127:1 (Message)

As in the parable above, the fourth seed that was planted landed on good ground and yielded hundredfold. The same applies to preparing the ground for a new building. Failure is guaranteed if the foundation is built on improperly prepared ground. Believe it or not, most new believers are not taught how to prepare their hearts to receive the seed. They are instructed how to be a "good" person, and how to be a "good" church member, but our Christian life has to be built on the "good" seed from Jesus.

Early in my Christian walk, I went on a mission trip to Peru to help in the construction of a church for the local missionary. At this time in my life, I had learned how to act as a "good Christian." I knew all the right things to say. I had it all down pat. I had seed, but it really was not good seed. The person that was supposed to translate for the pastor could not attend. All of a sudden, I found myself being the substitute translator. My communication skills in Spanish were very poor. There were times in my translation that I was preaching my own sermon because I did not know, nor was I capable of translating, the words in his vocabulary. Some of the words were colloquial southern words and expressions and I did not know the meaning of them. I certainly could not translate them into Spanish. He would use expressions like "can't never could," or "that dog won't hunt," or "the crimson blood of Christ." Huh? I assumed he meant red.

During that time, I thought I was serving God by "good" works, but suddenly I found myself in a testing of my faith. The pastor's sermon was about healing, so at the end of the message, he called for a laying of hands for those that were sick. On all of the mission trips that I served in Central and South America, I

If God doesn't build the house, the builders only build shacks. Psalms 127:1 (Message)

realized that when healing is preached, the people believe **IT WILL HAPPEN,** and they come to the altar to receive it. There is no doubt in their minds what God can do. A woman brought a baby who had open sores all over its body. When I saw the baby with all the sores, fear fell on me. The pastor wanted me to anoint with oil, lay hands, and pray for the baby in Spanish.

I refused to touch the baby. I remember telling the pastor that he should go ahead and lay hands on the child, and I would translate his prayer. He looked straight into my eyes, rebuking me and telling me to back off. He said there could be no lack of faith when asking God for healing. I received his rebuke because I knew the type of man he was and that he was right, and he pierced my heart with truth. Backing up to a wall on the back of the stage, I cried out to God, telling Him I was afraid I would catch the disease the baby had. I went as far as telling God that I did not believe He could protect me.

This was a point of testing my faith. God in His love and mercy looked beyond my fears and saw my sincerity. He intervened, filling me with His Spirit, and turned my fear into faith. Suddenly, I felt a warmth over my body, and I felt as if someone had grabbed me from the back of my shirt collar and supernaturally took a giant leap carrying me toward the front.

I ripped the baby from the pastor's arms, and I clenched the baby against my chest and anointed the baby with all that was within me. God took my lack of faith and my sincerity and He caused it to produce a good crop. It started as a reckless seed, but because of His compassion, He caused it to yield a good crop. I do not know what happened to the baby, but I believe that God is using him for such a time as this. I can say that this was a moment

If GOD doesn't build the house, the builders only build shacks. Psalms 127:1 (Message)

of healing for me. He healed my heart and gave me a compassion that I did not have.

The seed in my life germinated a tree that was growing up as a carnal man, but I thank God that his mercy endures forever and He pruned me of all the junk that I was enriching. The thing that I was lacking was preparation of the ground; I was not removing the detrimental parts of my life and replacing them with his Word. I was a content tree with green leaves that went to church and played the proper roles, but I was not producing fruit.

I am glad that although I deserved it, the Lord did not curse me as he did the fig tree of Mathew 21. Time and time again, I have to evaluate the soil where I am placed. Do I need to remove stumps? Do I need to compact the soil? If all I care about is just "good enough" and I am willing to live my life as a poor witness of a weak unconditioned life, then I will leave a Leaning Tower of Pisa testimony. A poor testament that **good enough is not good enough.**

*Song of Solomon 6:10 Who is she who looks forth as the morning, Fair as the moon, Clear as the sun, Awesome as an army with banners?*

The church! That is who; and I want to be a major part of her, carrying her banner, and preparing the way. Preparing the ground and removing unwanted matter, removing any foreign seeds that would choke the progress that would otherwise radiate a brightness. Plowing the ground and planting seeds everywhere I go. I want to be fair as the moon that I can have a natural attraction to the lost because they see Jesus and not me. I desire

If GOD doesn't build the house, the builders only build shacks. Psalms 127:1 (Message)

to be clear as the sun, that my life can radiate a life of love and compassion, not by becoming some religious fanatic, but by graciously loving people. I want to reflect a clearness of His love that others would not be blinded by the affairs of this world, but instead see Him. I want to be a soldier in His army carrying a banner that could only represent Him. I am glad that He has removed, and is still removing, unsuitable materials from my life, and that He is still working on me.

If GOD doesn't build the house, the builders only build shacks. Psalms 127:1 (Message)

~ Page 57 ~

Chapter 4

## *The Foundation*

*I Corinthians 3:11 (NIV) for no one can lay any foundation other than the one already laid, which is Jesus Christ.*

$\mathcal{I}$n the construction industry, the words foundation and footers are interchangeable and generally have the same meaning. Sometimes a building may be built on piles that are driven into the ground, other times the building may be constructed on a monolithic (cast as a single piece) slab and footing. To understand the distinction between them requires further explanation.

*Job 38:1 (KJV), Then the Lord answered Job out of the whirlwind, and said: Who is this who darkens counsel by words without knowledge? Now prepare yourself like a man; I will question you, and you shall answer Me. Where were you when I laid the foundations of the earth? Tell me, if you have understanding. Who determined its measurements? Surely you know! Or who stretched the line upon it? To what were its foundations fastened?*

If GOD doesn't build the house, the builders only build shacks. Psalms 127:1 (Message)

*Or who laid its cornerstone, when the morning stars sang together, and all the sons of God shouted for joy?*

God did not haphazardly lay the foundation of this world. He had measurements and gave an alignment of direction, and He anchored it down and established the point of beginning with the cornerstone. As God questioned Job, the same questions can be posed to us as we try to direct and confuse our own lives. It takes preparation, investigation, study, sanctification, and most of all surrender to Him, who knows all.

Foundations are not one-size-fits-all. The footing measurements are designed by a structural engineer and are based on the number of stories, the contributing weight of the building, and the load bearing capacity of the ground that will support it (remember the geotechnical engineer's report). In Job 38:1, we need to have understanding in order to determine the measurements of the foundation. We have to know the precise location of each footing as it is laid out by a surveyor, where the baseline and control point that becomes the corner stone will be set. Once all this is done, then we are able to determine how the foundation will bear on the ground below it.

Considering that the ground has now been adequately prepared for the building, the footing becomes an integral part of the structure's foundation... it is upon that which the building is built. There are several types of foundations, but for the purpose of this book, we will only discuss two: shallow and deep.

Shallow foundations, often called footings, are typically 18 inches high by 24 inches wide and can be continuous strips of

If GOD doesn't build the house, the builders only build shacks. Psalms 127:1 (Message)

~ Page 59 ~

concrete (grade beams) or they can be square or rectangular segments of concrete poured in place around the building used to transfer the weight from the supports to the earth. On the other hand, a deep foundation is necessary when the upper layer of earth is weak and will not support the load of a structure. Piles are driven down to the stronger layer of subsoil below that which is able to support the load resting on it and, in addition, the pile has a friction reaction force along its perimeter that assists in the load bearing capacity. Historically, piles are fabricated out of wood, steel, reinforced concrete, and pre-tensioned concrete.

Foundations, unlike many other parts of a structure, are hidden. They are tucked away below the ground, behind brick or stone, below flooring, and they do not get any recognition. As its name implies, however, it is the base upon which the building rests. In order for the rest of our lives to function properly (to be strong, solid, unshakeable), we have to build a sure and solid foundation that will last.

If God doesn't build the house, the builders only build shacks. Psalms 127:1 (Message)

To guarantee that a foundation will meet the guidelines for strength, it has to be free of inferior materials and foreign matter that will make it weak. Just as a structural engineer has guidelines to determine the dimensions of the foundation, we too have guidelines. In Job 38:1, God poses some questions: where were we when He laid out the foundation of the Earth? Who determined its measurements? How is our foundation fastened down? God is the one who laid out the foundations of the world, and it would be presumptuous of us to think that we can direct our lives. The Lord is our rock and fortress, our deliverer, our anchor, our strength. He is our tall tower and Him will I trust.

The foundation is simply a calculated mixture of suitable materials that interact together to create concrete. This concrete will be poured into the formwork that was laid out precisely as per the construction plans, and it will not flow out wildly seeking its own way and making its own direction. It has to be contained and has to have a specific layout so that it will work with the rest of the members that will depend on it. Before the concrete can be mixed and placed into the forms, an important element needs consideration.

Concrete acts best when it is under compression taking on a heavy load that pushes all the members to work close together in unison to resist whatever force acts upon it. It does not like to be pulled apart under tension that causes the members to be separated. For that reason, a key member is introduced, and that is the steel reinforcement bar, also known as rebar. The rebar allows the concrete to be rigid, yet flexible.

Since concrete is weaker in tension, the rebar is placed horizontally in the forms at designated areas for strength. In

If GOD doesn't build the house, the builders only build shacks. Psalms 127:1 (Message)

~ Page 61 ~

addition when the depth of the beam is restricted or where shear force is prevalent, a series of smaller bars wrap around the perimeter near the exterior of the beam, and they are closely spaced.

This is a beautiful picture of when a person is going through trials or stress: we as the body come close together, and we completely encompass him, providing him with prayer that will strengthen him.

There are reinforcement bars, known as vertical bars or  dowels, which are bent vertically in order to attach to the proposed columns or walls of the structure. The rebar allows for the concrete to have flexure and a grabbing effect. It has a characteristic and capability that, as Christians, we should want: to have a strong foundation while reaching out to others. The vertical rebar Christians should provide the connection with the other structural components and provide connections for future expansion.

*Ephesians 4:16 (NIV) From him the whole body, joined and held together by every supporting ligament, grows and builds itself up in love, as each part does its work.*

If GOD doesn't build the house, the builders only build shacks. Psalms 127:1 (Message)

~ Page 62 ~

The body of Christ should never be static (non-moving); it should make provisions for a dynamic church in spirit and in truth. The rebar is the methodology that allows one member of the body to be monolithic (cast as a single piece) with another member of the body. It is like the foot bone connected to the anklebone, etc., or the foundation connected to a column or a wall.

I learned the value of working together as a strong unit on a mission trip to Honduras. Our church sent a medical team to a small village in the mountains of Honduras to minister to the peoples' need and support a local missionary doctor. My wife signed me up for the trip because she knew that I would make a great addition to the team. I got angry with her for doing that and told her that I was an engineer, not a medic. Some minor medical training in the Air Force over 35 years ago did not qualify me for any position at a clinic. She insisted that I go because I was fluent in Spanish.

Again, I faced the dilemma of having a weak Spanish tongue, but this time mostly because I did not know the medical terms in English, much less in Spanish. As should be expected, the Lord intervened. What I was dreading to do turned into a fulfilling time in my life. As the people came in, we performed the typical triage examination. We asked them what their needs or ailments were and then I translated it to the doctor the best that I could. One specific moment an elderly lady walked in to our station and a young lady accompanied her.

I talked with the elderly woman (who I found to be the grandmother of this young lady) and she opened up about her granddaughter's life. In his wisdom, the missionary doctor

If GOD doesn't build the house, the builders only build shacks. Psalms 127:1 (Message)

provided me with a smock that made me appear as if I was a legitimate physician, which perhaps caused the grandmother to confide in me. I learned that the young lady had been abandoned by both of her parents at a very young age. Her father was physically and emotionally abusive with her. She was passed around from family member to family member, and each time she was oppressed and abused. The grandmother proceeded to reveal to me that the young lady's uncle was abusing her inappropriately and this had happened with other family members including her own father. Several times, I tried to get the young lady to talk to me, and she would reject and not look at me.

This young lady had such wounds that no physician in this world could help her. Only the Great Physician could do such a miracle for this young lady. The Holy Spirit used my lips of clay to speak to her about her Heavenly Father. I shared the love of God with her, and I told her that men that are on this earth, including me, may let her down, but that her Heavenly Father would never abandon her nor hurt her in any way. The Holy Spirit used me to build a foundation in her life that she would be able to stand upon.

After the doctor examined her and they were ready to leave, I took a risk and grabbed her hand and prayed with her. As I finished praying, she looked up and smiled at me. I told her that she was precious in God's eyes and He would never leave her nor forsake her. As they left, the doctor and I cried because our hearts were so broken. They got halfway down the room and she turned around and ran to me and embraced me. I knew that in her heart she had seen the love of the Father for the first time. What the devil tried to destroy through the men in her life, God rebuilt using

If God doesn't build the house, the builders only build shacks. Psalms 127:1 (Message)

another man.  God, using me as a vessel, was able to build a foundation of love, joy, peace in her life.  Against such a foundation there is no law and God built it, through a yielded vessel. From that point on, I looked forward to the trips each year. God allowed me to become a rebar that joined one member of the body (the doctors) with another member (His children) in Honduras, and to offer them more than medical treatment: a solid foundation in Christ.

Following a discussion of how critical it is to prepare the ground, the subject of preparing a proper concrete mix for the foundation arises.  The construction of a sure foundation, one that is able to support great loads, one that will withstand storms, and one that will endure the test of time, has to consist of a specific formula of quality ingredients.  From a human perspective, the only foundation that we should build upon is Christ Himself. Being a carpenter by trade as told in Mark 6:3, Jesus had a working knowledge about construction and its materials.  He was familiar with wood, brick, mortar, and essential tools, and He recognized which materials were suitable and which He would reject.

*I  Corinthians  12:12(NIV)  For as the body  is  one and has many members, but all the members of that one body, being many, are one body, so also is Christ.*

When considering the above passage as it relates to the physical body, reflect for a moment on how people of many races, (cultures, age, gender, personalities, education, socio-economic positions, etc.) in the world make up the body of Christ.  Each member should have the same care one for another because as

If GOD doesn't build the house, the builders only build shacks. Psalms 127:1 (Message)

one member suffers, all the members help to bear the burden. If one member is honored, all the members rejoice with him. For instance, if you lose your job, your family (the church) bears your distress with you by showing support in any way possible. On the other hand, when a member gets a huge promotion, we become ecstatic and celebrate with him. Both responses require unison with the body. When analyzing what makes the foundation strong, it is determined by the composition of the concrete.

In the body of Christ, unity and diversity are fundamental, but without division among the members. One member of a body does not make the whole; it is made up of many distinct members. Each member possesses his or her own position, shape, use, etc. Some have one gift and others a different one. Variety in the physical body along with the body of Christ contributes to the beauty and strength of it. The ingredients, once combined, all work together to give the concrete its durability, longevity and strength.

The right mix of concrete is necessary for the construction of a footing, a grade beam, a wall, a piling, or a concrete slab. Individual components of the mix are chosen for quality. This mix is a conglomerate of coarse aggregates (gravel), sand, cement, water, and special chemical agents. The specific formula for the

If GOD doesn't build the house, the builders only build shacks. Psalms 127:1 (Message)

concrete mix is based on proper ratios of each necessary material that will yield the design strength. We also must have the proper ratio of water in the mixture to allow it to be workable and not too stiff. There will be strain when the mix is too stiff and it will prevent the members from spreading it fast enough within the forms. It will harden too quickly and, as a result, create cold joints, joints that will not let one section adhere with another.

When we do not allow others to work with us, we create cold boundaries; maybe we unintentionally give them a cold shoulder. If we are not careful, we can become a stiff-necked and callused people that will prevent a monolithic pour, or a close bond.

On the other hand, if too much water is added, there is no control forming the concrete. The result is a weak concrete with honeycomb voids. We have to allow ourselves to be manageable; not running out of control doing our own thing that ultimately create voids in our lives. The right mix will function most effectively in the Kingdom of God.

As discussed previously, the coarse aggregate portion of the mix is what Jesus was referring to a rock upon which He will build His Church. To understand how to make the body of Christ strong is to realize and appreciate contributions by each individual member.

The church is composed of parts that vary in characteristics, just as in the mix for concrete. The more spread the gradation, the stronger the body becomes as it works together in harmony. As 1 Corinthians 12:27 confirms, we are the body of Christ and individual members.

If GOD doesn't build the house, the builders only build shacks. Psalms 127:1 (Message)

~ Page 67 ~

*1 Corinthians 12:27-28 (NKJV), [27] now you are the body of Christ, and members individually. [28] And God has appointed these in the church: first apostles, second prophets, third teachers, after that miracles, then gifts of healings, helps, administrations, varieties of tongues.*

As God calls members to serve where He pleases, the rock size will decrease and each member will fulfill his or her intended purpose. The gradation of the aggregate in no way correlates to the significance of the calling from God. It is simply a designation of position. The larger rocks over the ages have been formed and sealed from smaller aggregates. They are strong and large in stature, tried by the burdens of life, and while they may seem to use a larger percentage of the mix, they are fewer in number.

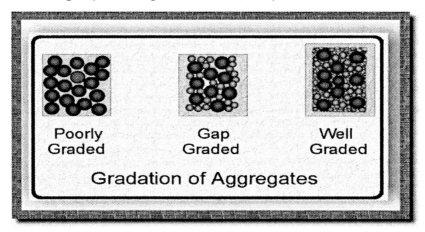

Poorly Graded    Gap Graded    Well Graded

**Gradation of Aggregates**

Because they realize their place in the mix, they lead not as tyrants, but like gentle lions that protect and shape others.

In the passage above, God first appoints the apostle. This is not a common word used in today's church. People mainly associate it to the 12 disciples. The word apostle is derived from

If GOD doesn't build the house, the builders only build shacks. Psalms 127:1 (Message)

~ Page 68 ~

the Greek *apostolos*, meaning "one who is sent." This is why Paul also had this title. In the modern church world, an apostle could be church-planters and missionaries. This selection of coarse aggregates consists of the pastors, evangelists, teachers, and any ministers of God's Word that are bold, strong, edifying, yet gentle and compassionate of others.

They are constantly looking for the smaller members, as a shepherd would tend to his sheep. He protects those surrounding Him as they support Him.

As the gradation becomes smaller, there is a move from the adults to youth. Teenagers have a place in the Kingdom that no one else can fill. They offer the excitement of a child mixed with the yearning to be an adult. When nurtured from childhood with the greatness of God, the forgiveness from Jesus and the alliance with the Holy Spirit, teenagers become invincible. Take, for example, the story of how a teenager, filled with the Spirit of God, was able to bring down a giant with a simple slingshot and a stone that the Lord provided. Although he did not have the experience that the more mature aggregate had, he allowed himself to be used by God. I believe that a teenager filled with the Spirit and the anointing of God can change the world.

Another example of a young person in the Bible that played a major role in the Kingdom of God was Miriam, the sister of Moses. Miriam, in her quick thinking, not only saved her brother's life, but she saved an entire nation. When Pharaoh's daughter pulled Moses out of the river, Miriam was there. She arranged a Hebrew nurse for baby Moses that just happened to be his mother. She, too, allowed herself to be a productive member of the Kingdom without even realizing the magnitude of it.

If GOD doesn't build the house, the builders only build shacks. Psalms 127:1 (Message)

The most treasured teenager in the Bible has to be Mary, mother of Jesus. She willingly became a teenage mother and raised the Son of God at the expense of disgrace from her hometown. Mary realized the immeasurable responsibility in this calling and I believe she instilled in Him a love for His Father and compassion for others that so shaped His life.

In 1809, a baby boy was born in Coupvray, France. As he grew older, he often spent time playing close to his father's shop where there were dangerous tools, so his father was protective of him and looked out for him. Just like most of us that are told to flee all appearance of evil, he was warned often not to touch his father's tools. Nevertheless, the temptation was too strong and it overcame him. One day, when no one was looking, the three-year-old boy picked up a sharp knife and he tried to cut a piece of leather. The cutting knife blade slid, and it gouged one of his eyes. Because medical care was not adequate in those days, the wound became dangerously infected and spread to his good eye. The boy was now blind. It did not, however, stop him from exceling as he attended the Royal Institute for Blind Youth in Paris. Most of us have a tendency that as soon as we encounter a deterrent, we give up and give way and surrender.

As a young man at the institute, he invented a system of reading and writing for the blind that involved raised dots, which was named after him, Louis Braille. At age 19, Braille became a full-time teacher at the Royal Institute for Blind Youth, where he remained until his death at age 43. What the adversary (the devil) set out to destroy, God in his loving mercy turned into a success for those that are not able to see with their natural eyes.

If GOD doesn't build the house, the builders only build shacks. Psalms 127:1 (Message)

Today, Braille is a universally used tactile method of writing and reading for the blind. Louis developed tuberculosis and as he lay dying he said, "God was pleased to hold before my eyes the dazzling

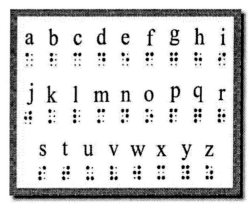

splendors of eternal hope. After that, doesn't it seem that nothing more could keep me bound to the earth?"(7) What a tremendous testimony that the loss of sight of one man allows others to see, read and understand by using the sense of feeling. He may have been a teenager when he invented the Braille system, but he was an aggregate that allowed himself to be used in the mix. In the mix of the Kingdom, God used these smaller teenage rocks to accomplish His will, and He wants to do the same today.

Today's youth are full of energy with dreams that need the trust and encouragement from the rest of the mix to provide the strength they can contribute. God intends for the mix to be well gradated.

*Mathew 19: 14 (NIV) "Let the little children come to me, and do not hinder them, for the kingdom of heaven belongs to such as these."*

As the size of the aggregate in the mix is becoming smaller, we next consider children. They were special to Jesus as

If GOD doesn't build the house, the builders only build shacks. Psalms 127:1 (Message)

~ Page 71 ~

part of the mix because He knew they had hearts from seeds of "good ground." A small child has the same effect on us. They are carefree. They have no worry, anxiety, or stress. And they are free as birds. Little children are major contributors to the Kingdom of God. Their faith is great, and we are to see the harvest coming from children as they grow in the Lord. Take, for example, the feeding of the 5,000, also known as the "miracle of the five loaves and two fish" given in the Gospel of John. He tells how five barley loaves and two small fish supplied by a boy were used by Jesus to feed a multitude. The disciples wanted to send this mob of people away because evening was approaching and they were in a remote place where food and supplies were not available.

Jesus was not concerned that there were no supermarkets close by. He simply told the disciples to give the people something to eat. Perhaps at this point they had forgotten all the miracles that Jesus had performed. Andrew went as far as asking, "How are five loaves and two fish going to feed this multitude?" But this little child recognized that he was in the presence of the miracle-worker. The child gave them to Jesus, Jesus gave them to the disciples, and the disciples gave them to the people. They all ate and were satisfied, and the disciples picked up 12 baskets of broken pieces that were left over. The number of those who ate was about 5,000 men, besides women and children. A little child has great faith: they simply believe with no questions asked, and no complexities of issues that this world hurls against us.

Every size of the aggregate is crucial to obtain the required strength. Think of how a small pebble represents the infants. They occupy those cavities that larger stones are unable to fill.

If GOD doesn't build the house, the builders only build shacks. Psalms 127:1 (Message)

One may think that a baby does not have any direct effect nor contribute to the Kingdom, but the fact of the matter is that a baby always seems to stop everyone. They draw people in with their cooing, smiling, and gentle hand and feet gestures. You may have had a bad day, but an infant in your arms makes you forget all the troubles of this world. I have been going through a difficult time in my professional career and have been ready to relocate to another place from where I am now, but my granddaughter was just born, and as I get around her I forget about my problems. I am not as interested in my career. I do not want to relocate, and perhaps she is helping me to put life in perspective and set priorities. I want to be as close to her as God will allow me. I know this: that as we give them back to the parent, we walk away with a smile. They are like a medicine to the heart. After all, God's plan for redemption of humanity began with a baby!

The smallest component of the dry aggregate ingredients to consider is the sand. It fills the spaces between the larger rocks. In the Kingdom of God, the sand is the people that think they may not have a special talent or gift to serve in the Kingdom; that they are so small and insignificant that they do not matter. The fact is that God did not create any wasted by-products. He uses all of us, even when it may seem insignificant to us. He tells in 1 Corinthians that we are all honored. Without the sand, the mix will have a great void ratio; there would be gaps allowing air in that would make the concrete mixture weak.

Without the sand-type Christians, the enemy will sneak into a cavity that looks small and insignificant. Then he can attack and make the body ineffective and weak. The sand-type Christians are reliable. They blend in with others and work in

If GOD doesn't build the house, the builders only build shacks. Psalms 127:1 (Message)

~ Page 73 ~

multiple capacities. They fill in all the ministries that the staff cannot and they probably do not realize how much the staff is blessed by them. They turn on the lights. They turn the air conditioning unit on so that the rest of us are comfortable. As small as their ministry may seem, without the sand-type Christians, the mixture would not yield the strength needed for the final result.

After all the aggregates are added, cement is the next property of the mix to consider. Cement is manufactured in Portland through a closely controlled chemical combination of calcium, silicon, aluminum, iron and other chemicals. The materials are placed in a cement kiln and heated to about 2,700 degrees Fahrenheit. The use of cement in construction can be traced back to the Romans who used burnt lime as a binder. Just like cement, the Son of God represents the substance that has been tried by fire and found to be pure.

*Daniel 3:25 (NKJV), "Look!" he answered, I see four men loose, walking in the midst of the fire; and they are not hurt, and the form of the fourth is like the Son of God.*

The cement is that ingredient in the fiery furnace when Jesus appeared with Shadrach, Meshach, and Abed-Nego. He was their deliverer, and the refuge we can trust to bring us through the fire. The cement that saturates the Lord provides the glue that binds us together. When we are weak as an estranged mix, He is the agent to make us strong. He is the cement with a chemical composition that causes the interaction with the mix to form a strong and a well-gradated body. Without the cement, we

If GOD doesn't build the house, the builders only build shacks. Psalms 127:1 (Message)

~ Page 74 ~

would be a bunch of members independently laying around, not adhering to each other, and with no clear direction as to our place in the body.

The final ingredient in the mixture of concrete is water. I relate water to the Holy Spirit. He functions as a catalyst in our lives. When He indwells us, He begins the work of revealing the truth in the Word. He teaches us to produce love, joy, peace, patience, kindness, goodness, faithfulness, gentleness, and self-control. He reveals to us that these are not works of our flesh, which are incapable of producing a solid foundation, but they are products of the Spirit's presence in our lives. Concrete is formed when the water is mixed with the cement that creates a paste that binds the sand and aggregates together and hardens. Therefore, for us, when the Holy Spirit waters the surface of our lives, He brings adhesion between all the members of the mix that are ready to become strong and fulfill their purpose. The cement pastes adheres quickly and satisfactorily to a wet surface more so than to a dry surface, thus the need to keep the Holy Spirit near to us as a Church.

*Isaiah 44:3 (NKJV), For I will pour water on him who is thirsty, and floods on the dry ground; I will pour My Spirit on your descendants, and My blessing on your offspring;*

Once the water is added to the aggregates, sand, and cement, the mixture starts to harden quickly and become strong. All Portland cements are set and harden through a chemical reaction with water called hydration. During this reaction, an attraction forms on the surface of each cement particle. He

If GOD doesn't build the house, the builders only build shacks. Psalms 127:1 (Message)

knows the proper amount of water to add: too much will cause the mix to be too watery and lose strength; not enough makes the mixture difficult to handle and hydration will set in too fast. Once the concrete is thoroughly mixed and workable, it will be placed in forms before the mixture becomes too stiff. Additional water may be needed to ensure workability of the concrete, to facilitate placing it in the desired position.

We need to stay in tune with Him to learn to obtain the right mix with the proper amount of ingredients. If we get too religious (watered down) then chances are we become like the Sanhedrin, so heavenly-minded that we are no earthly good. If we have too little religion, we become hard, callused, secluded, and difficult to be close to, and we will not bond well with others. We have a tendency to run off relationships and friendships that want to be there in the mix to make our lives more complete. The attraction in the body of God should be one that grows and expands until it links up with other members.

During placement, the concrete is consolidated, shaken through a vibration process to compact it within the forms. This process is necessary to eliminate potential flaws, such as honeycombs and air pockets. We all have flaws that we allow to develop throughout our Christian walk; therefore there is a sanctification process that has to occur to eliminate flaws that would make the structure weak. For slabs, concrete is left to stand until the surface moisture film disappears, then a wood or metal hand float is used to smooth off the concrete. For Christians, relationships with others can provide this process. For example, it has been said that with men, iron sharpens iron.

If GOD doesn't build the house, the builders only build shacks. Psalms 127:1 (Message)

Caring and sharing life's issues and burdens with one another creates a strong bond.

The final step in ensuring the concrete is strong is the curing process. Curing keeps the recently poured concrete from drying out too quickly by covering the surface with water to keep it moist. Proper curing ensures the continued hydration of the cement so that the concrete continues to gain strength. This step is vital because this causes the surface to be strong, and it allows the ingredients to completely bond. It will prevent cracks and seal those voids where the enemy wants to penetrate our lives. If this process is neglected, there is irreparable loss of strength in the concrete. Water (the Holy Spirit) is the component used for the hydration of the cementing materials to set and harden during the

period of curing. The sufficiently hardened foundation surface will be protected from marring or will keep hurts from entering. This is like putting on the whole armor of God to protect our hearts and to prevent a fiery dart from piercing our bodies. Putting on this armor is like **Armor All ™**, which prevents cracking on any piece of furniture, including our cars. We apply it to prevent premature aging and to protect it from the dehydration of the sun. Special techniques are used for curing concrete during extremely cold or hot weather to protect the concrete.

If GOD doesn't build the house, the builders only build shacks. Psalms 127:1 (Message)

Contrary to those who think they are no longer of any use when they reach their senior years, concrete continues to get stronger as it ages. Most of the hydration and strength gained take place within the first month of concrete's life cycle, but hydration continues at a slower rate for many years.

Getting the desired strength of concrete is not always easy. Sometimes it means combining many different ingredients that do not seem like obvious choices, but in the end are exactly right in combination and in perfect harmony with each other. Sometimes you make a batch and realize it is not giving the results that are specified by the designer. Sometimes it takes remixing until we get it right. God wants us to work together, to resolve our differences, and expand our similarities in such a way that our world is a better place and we fulfill His will.

It is not always easy, but a strong final mix makes all the hard work and harmonious labor worthwhile. None of us is enough, in and of ourselves. We must work together, and sometimes work really **HARD**, to get the right mix that results in the desired end product.

*Matthew 7:24-27 (NKJV)* ²⁴ *"Therefore whoever hears these sayings of Mine, and does them, I will liken him to a wise man who built his house on the rock:* ²⁵ *and the rain descended, the floods came, and the winds blew and beat on that house; and it did not fall, for it was founded on the rock.* ²⁶ *But everyone who hears these sayings of mine, and does not do them, will be like a foolish man who built his house on the sand:*
²⁷ *and the rain descended, the floods came, and the winds blew and beat on that house; and it fell. And great was its fall."*

If GOD doesn't build the house, the builders only build shacks. Psalms 127:1 (Message)

This scripture always drove me crazy because I had such a deviation with it. I learned in my professional training that a structure can be built on sand and that it would be very strong. If you drive along coastal areas, you will see that there are many high-rise buildings built along sandy beaches. A house or a building may be built on sand and it would be very strong and the foundation may be able to sustain the loads that are imposed on it. Such a structure built on the sand may sustain the torrential rains that can fall on it. It may withstand the lateral winds that put immense pressure on it, even perhaps from a hurricane.

But one day I realized that the writer was not caught by surprise. The writer had an insight on deep foundations that I was missing. We cannot outsmart God. He can allow a storm like Katrina to be let loose, and no matter how well the foundation was constructed, it will snatch it away.

After Katrina was over, there were buildings snatched up and moved to a different location. I saw piles that were once driven deep into the sand that were now uprooted. Sometimes it is much easier to build on a solid rock: it requires less preparation, it costs less, and it will surely be load bearing on its own without the benefit of any additional  preparation. Deep foundations are those that have to penetrate the soil strata to a great depth. They may be piles that have to be

If GOD doesn't build the house, the builders only build shacks. Psalms 127:1 (Message)

~ Page 79 ~

hammered into the ground with a lot of force. They may be helical anchors (metal screwing anchors) that can resist heavy loads or uplift.

I have a tendency to want to do things the hard way. Yes, I can build the house on sand, but it takes a great deal of extra effort and expense that may not be a very "wise" move. Yes, it can be built on a piling system that has to be penetrated to a depth that may resist the forces of the load. Too often in my life, instead of listening to His words and doing His command, I depend on my abilities, my knowledge, and consequently unexpected problems pop up.

The children of Israel did not always heed His Word. They went about doing things with their own understanding and caused a great deal of time loss. You can say, perhaps, we can get to the ultimate place more than one way, but it is also wise to redeem the time that the Lord has loaned us in this world and avoid those things that can cause us heartache and stress. There are other times when we are doing all that has been commanded of us, yet life makes excessive demands, and some we bring upon ourselves. A deep pile is designed to sustain the loads that a normal shallow footing could not. However, even though they are driven to refusal (the point where they cannot penetrate any more), it is possible that exterior sideways forces can appear and weaken them.

Provisions have to be made by providing a batter pile, an additional pile that is driven diagonally to help carry the load imposed on the pile. It is a pile that will shore up and give greater stability.

If GOD doesn't build the house, the builders only build shacks. Psalms 127:1 (Message)

~ Page 80 ~

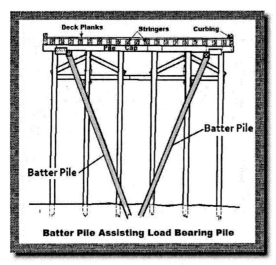

Batter Pile Assisting Load Bearing Pile

In our lives, we may be very strong, but there are times that stress due to unforeseen forces arises when we least expect it. God, in his mercy, makes a provision and adds a batter pile, someone who will come to help and share the burden.

A pile cap is restrained on the two piles interconnecting them and making them accountable for each other. This concept is similar to the concept in the Bible where a yoke of oxen ties two oxen together.

In the Old Testament the yoke was used to subjugate or force into human labor or enslave someone. However, whatever the work was, it was done alone, and the load was not shared with others. In the New Testament, a yoke was a crossbar that encircled the necks of a pair of oxen or mules to allow them to share the load. Jesus is a help mate working alongside me. He encourages me, and He leads me so I do not go astray. I can find rest because He makes my burden light. As it said in Deuteronomy, one can chase a thousand to flight; two can chase ten thousand to flight. It is amazing how two piles can carry a much greater load than

If GOD doesn't build the house, the builders only build shacks. Psalms 127:1 (Message)

each one independently. With God, the possibilities are endless. Just for fun, let me illustrate this in a calculus equation. If "x" represents a positive rational number (God) and "c" represents any real number (us), as x approaches Infinity ($\infty$), in other words as x gets larger and larger in the fraction, and as long as God is on the bottom, and we are on top dictating our own lives, then our possibilities will approach zero (0). We set our ways higher than his ways.

$$\lim_{x \to \infty} \frac{c}{x} = 0 \quad \textbf{Possibilities are finite}$$

On the other hand, as "x" approaches infinity and God is on top and in control, and "c" is on the bottom, and we are humbling ourselves and being directed by him, it does not matter how much we do, because whatever we do will never approach him who is **infinite**. He is still in control and, as we seek after him, our possibilities are **endless**.

$$\lim_{x \to \infty} \frac{x}{c} = \infty \quad \textbf{Possibilities are infinite}$$

Yes, a structure can be built on sand, but who knows what problems can be encountered in the process? There can be a vibratory uplift of the pile, false reading in the refusal bearing capacity of the pile or an excessive amount of concrete pumped into an auger cast pile. All these can be hidden issues for the stability and strength of a pile. The Lord has foreknowledge of all the adversity we will face in our lives. He knows the right time and

If GOD doesn't build the house, the builders only build shacks. Psalms 127:1 (Message)

the right location to build: the places that will keep us from those annoying unwanted encounters of life.

*Psalm 18:2 The Lord is my rock, my fortress and my deliverer; my God is my rock, in whom I take refuge, my shield and the horn of my salvation, my stronghold.*

It would be more feasible to build on a rock formation where the builder already has knowledge, experience, and insight to keep us out of trouble. Working with Him on our side, we will avoid any alluvial (unwanted muck) soils that soften our stability in building a solid structure on a solid foundation.

He is our foundation. He is our rock. He is our stability. He is my strong hold, and He is the one that will hold us steady if we begin to sink, settle, or fail. With God controlling the environment that we are in, the possibilities are unending.

If GOD doesn't build the house, the builders only build shacks. Psalms 127:1 (Message)

~ Page 83 ~

Chapter 5

# The Materials

*1 Corinthians 3:9-15 ⁹ for we are God's fellow workers; you are God's field, you are God's building. ¹⁰ According to the grace of God which was given to me, as a wise master builder I have laid the foundation, and another builds on it. But let each one take heed how he builds on it. ¹¹ For no other foundation can anyone lay than that which is laid, which is Jesus Christ. ¹² Now if anyone builds on this foundation with gold, silver, precious stones, wood, hay, straw, ¹³ each one's work will become clear; for the Day will declare it, because it will be revealed by fire; and the fire will test each one's work, of what sort it is. ¹⁴ If anyone's work which he has built on it endures, he will receive a reward. ¹⁵ If anyone's work is burned, he will suffer loss; but he himself will be saved, yet so as through fire.*

*N*ow that a sure foundation has been laid, the concrete has cured to its full strength, and the rebar has been placed purposely to connect with the columns, the building materials for the structure can be purchased and delivered. Any person who has ever constructed any sort of structure realizes that the

If GOD doesn't build the house, the builders only build shacks. Psalms 127:1 (Message)

~ Page 84 ~

completed product will only be as strong as the individual materials selected. Crooked 2x4's or cheap plywood may get the job done, but eventually the building will suffer and repairs will have to be made.

I am sure that you are familiar with the phrase "you get what you pay for." In construction, the idea is for a building to last at least its design cycle, and cheap materials may not meet that qualification. That being said, construction materials have to stand the test of time as they are exposed to the elements. There is also the consideration of how construction materials can vary in different areas of the country.

We live in Florida so it is customary here for buildings near the ocean or the gulf to be built using materials that are hurricane and salt resistant. Even the windows and doors have a specific strength rating depending on how far the structure is located from the coastline. Structures in hot or humid atmospheres need low maintenance materials that are resistant to salt air and, in the case of those structures that are constructed out of timber, their materials must be protected against the infestation of termites that would barrage and debilitate them.

California is an area that is earthquake prone with building code mandates that the type and strength of the materials used be able to withstand seismic movement. The best of designs and construction cannot be proven, though, until tested. The structural engineer specifies materials that have been tested by the American Society of Testing Materials (ASTM) to withstand the magnitude of the forces. ASTM tests the materials for different properties, and assures that the particular use of different materials meets the specified requirements.

If GOD doesn't build the house, the builders only build shacks. Psalms 127:1 (Message)

For example, materials used where rust would be prominent may require a coating for cathodic protection (CP) as outlined per ASTM. Cathodic protection is a method used to control corrosion of a metal. I find it fascinating that one way that cathodic protection works is to tie the metal to be protected with a **"sacrificial metal"** to act as an anode. This is a perfect picture of how Jesus became the sacrificial metal to protect me from my **condemnation, corrosion, and corruption.**

The verse in 1 Corinthians is a classic contrast of construction and the Christian life. In the scripture above, it first appeared to me that Paul was building with six different types of

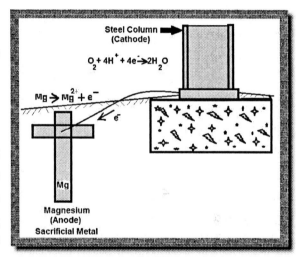

materials. As I studied the scripture closer, I noticed that he actually indicated that there are only two types of materials to choose from; they are costly or cheap, permanent or temporary. These materials have to be worthy of the structure that is being built. They must be of the type that will endure a fire and the test of time. Unlike the gold, silver, and precious stones, "wood, hay, and straw" are substandard materials because they will not be able to stand the testing of fire. They are unfit for a long-lasting construction project. These are the perishable materials that the carnal person would find adequate.

If GOD doesn't build the house, the builders only build shacks. Psalms 127:1 (Message)

Paul instructs us to use the best materials; long-lasting ones that will endure, and not cheap, temporal, and flammable ones. The unfortunate fact is that we live in a society where appearance plays a major role. As long as something is built to look good, it does not matter whether or not the quality is everlasting. It is not so much different for some Christians as they live their lives in the same manner. It is such a fallacy that as long as others think that we are doing well, we are completely satisfied and living a victorious life. A marriage may be falling apart, but as long as the couple can enter the church services with a smile on their faces, the crumbling materials (broken hearts) on the inside will not show. Paul emphasizes the truth that one day, despite our hidden secrets or unknown activities, Christ will judge our work. As a result, each person will be rewarded according to his efforts in building up of the body.

The purpose of the testing is to give an inspection of the worker as to the nature of our work. It is not a disapproval of the worker. Romans 8 tells us that there is no condemnation for those who seek the Lord; the test is for our measure of reward in heaven. It is reasonable to understand that cutting corners and using cheap materials will also have its reward. The worker loses the potential reward they might have received for the poorly performed work using poorly chosen materials.

*Ezekiel 13:10-12(NIV) Because they lead my people astray, saying, "Peace," when there is no peace, and because, when a flimsy wall is built, they cover it with whitewash, [11] therefore tell those who cover it with whitewash that it is going to fall. Rain will come in torrents, and I will send*

If GOD doesn't build the house, the builders only build shacks. Psalms 127:1 (Message)

~ Page 87 ~

*hailstones hurtling down, and violent winds will burst forth.*
*¹² When the wall collapses, will people not ask you, "Where is the*
*whitewash you covered it with?"*

The wall that Ezekiel is referencing was not built with the correct building materials and yet the implication is that the builder knows what is on the inside but does not care. The presentation and image that we may portray will not immediately reveal that we are building flimsy walls, built just to get by. The only true test to show the quality of materials will come in the form of adversity: rain, hailstones, and violent winds. These remove the whitewash to expose the true ingredients used and will determine if the wall stands or falls. Sometimes failure to build with adequate materials will not be seen for many years, but it will always reveal itself.

*Matthew 23:26-28(NKJV) ²⁶ Blind Pharisee, first cleanse*
*the inside of the cup and dish, that the outside of them may be*
*clean also.²⁷ Woe to you, scribes and Pharisees, hypocrites! For*
*you are like whitewashed tombs which indeed appear beautiful*
*outwardly, but inside are full of dead men's bones and all*
*uncleanness. ²⁸ Even so you also outwardly appear righteous to*
*men, but inside you are full of hypocrisy and lawlessness.*

Why are so many Christians putting up a facade that everything is well, yet within the interior, their lives are falling apart? What materials are being used to build our lives? Could it be we are building the inside of a structure with materials borrowed from others?

If GOD doesn't build the house, the builders only build shacks. Psalms 127:1 (Message)

In our inner being, we live an unclean life full of dead men's bones. We come to a Sunday morning church service and build our entire Christian walk on one sermon from the pastor. Since I am an engineer, my profession is about numbers and formulas, so let's look at some numbers and see how we stand up as Sunday morning Christians. I will keep it simple. There are 8,760 hours in a year, and if we receive one hour of the Gospel 52 times a year, that means that we are only getting 0.6 % hour of the Gospel on a yearly basis. With internet capability on smart phones, along with tablets, laptops and the "old" PC, social media including Facebook, Tumblr, Instagram, Twitter, and others (8), occupies an average of 3.2 hours per day, which equates to 13.36% of yearly total time. In order to build a solid relationship with the Lord, the comparison of 0.6% to 13.36%, would be much skewed. If we devote such a small amount of time to our relationship with God, why do we expect Him to give us big results?

The walls that we build in our relationship with Him will be able to stand when the storms come if we build them in Him, with His materials. There are no fake substitutes in the building process and there are no shortcuts. There is no such thing as a drive-thru relationship with Him, no fast food served on Sunday morning. It takes work, relationship, and study to be able to understand what materials the designer specifies for our lives. If the designer specified a 2x6 treated stud, it would be presumptuous of us to think that the designer did not know what he was doing and choose to build it with a 2x4 untreated stud instead.

The master builder has a purpose for what He has laid out in our lives. He knows what the end result is going to yield and He

If God doesn't build the house, the builders only build shacks. Psalms 127:1 (Message)

has laid the foundation. All we have to do is to build on it as He instructs. One thing I have learned over the years is that lost people analyze Christians for answers. They may be going astray, and it may not seem like it, but they look to us for peace and answers. The world has a close eye on us and it wants to see if the whitewash that we may have on the outside will come off and reveal a counterfeit.

When I was in college, I led a Bible study with several Christian students. Since we did not have smart phones with Bible apps, I carried my big, black leather Bible to our Bible study. While I gave no reason to doubt otherwise, I guess that carrying a large Bible made it easy to identify me as a Christian. In my dormitory, there was a group of guys that made fun of me, no matter where I was. Whenever they saw me coming, they chanted, "Here comes the preacher, here comes the preacher. Preach it, brother, preach it." Their chant did not bother me, because I knew who I represented, and the message I brought was a message of hope and peace. One day, one of the young men came up to me and asked to speak with me. He told me how sick his mother was, and he asked me to pray for her. I prayed with the young man about his mom's sickness, but also led him in a sinners' prayer. I remember him telling me that he could only turn to me, because he believed that I knew God and that I would speak to God on his mother's behalf. Now keep in mind that I am not now, nor was I then, an ordained minister. I was simply a man that loved the Lord. The young man must have recognized that, because when he approached me, he did not ask me for my religious credentials.

The world is not interested in our religious pedigree. It is looking for answers, which only come from above. This world is

If GOD doesn't build the house, the builders only build shacks. Psalms 127:1 (Message)

in need of someone that will intercede on its behalf. So many times I remind myself that, like Job, I have an intercessor that sits at the right hand of God, and He is my advocate that is pleading my case before the throne room of heaven.

I could have reacted negatively to the barrage of mocking and ridicule from those young men, but I am grateful to God that the materials that I was using to build my life were pure and I was able to share with another.

*Ezekiel 13:13-15(NIV) Therefore this is what the Sovereign LORD says: In my wrath I will unleash a violent wind, and in my anger hailstones and torrents of rain will fall with destructive fury. 14 I will tear down the wall you have covered with whitewash and will level it to the ground so that its foundation will be laid bare. When it falls, you will be destroyed in it; and you will know that I am the LORD.*

*15 So I will pour out my wrath against the wall and against those who covered it with whitewash. I will say to you, "The wall is gone and so are those who whitewashed it..."*

In verse 15, the Lord deals with the building of a wall. Whether this is a literal wall or an application to the wickedness of the prophets, there is much here for us to apply to our lives. We are the materials that God uses to build his Church, and because He so passionately cares for mankind, He provides every avenue to ensure we have acceptable materials for building. Unfortunately, because of our human nature, sin (bad material) continues to be covered up with whitewash. God is a merciful God, but He will not be mocked. Luke 12:2 confirms this: "For

If GOD doesn't build the house, the builders only build shacks. Psalms 127:1 (Message)

~ Page 91 ~

there is nothing covered that will not be revealed, nor hidden that will not be known." We are to use the best materials to build, so when the violent storm is unleashed on our lives, what is revealed will be saved.

Have you ever worked on a project in which things just did not seem to go the way you planned? Something goes wrong with the material; parts are lost or broken, and the quality is substandard. We do the same thing to God. We disobey, we get lost or broken, we procrastinate, we do not study, and then we fail to complete. The process with God is different, though. He does not throw up His hands and say, "Forget it! It is hopeless! They are hopeless and worthless! I cannot continue building anymore!" No! He is the master builder. As long as the foundation was constructed well, and as long as the proper materials have been made available, God will continue to build and complete His masterpiece. God is the "architect and builder." We have to allow God to tear down the walls that have been poorly built. If we are part of a complacent attitude, building with poor materials and without care, then He will take the walls down to the ground and its foundation will be the only thing remaining. He will rebuild, and He will find someone that will be obedient to him and who will follow the plans for the building. I am talking about a new structure, a new building, and a new creation!

There is a new city; a new Jerusalem God wants to build in us. He is not just going to renovate, or rebuild from an old city. He is not going to borrow leftover scraps or second-hand materials. When we repent, we believe and claim Jesus as our Savior and Lord. Old building materials will pass away and, behold, we will be reconstructed by his hands and become new.

If GOD doesn't build the house, the builders only build shacks. Psalms 127:1 (Message)

Our old work of unbelief or other beliefs will be torn away and discarded. God will now build on the foundation of our new life in Christ. **WE ARE NOW UNDER NEW CONSTRUCTION!** He will change our lives if we allow Him, and for most of us, it will not be an easy process. There will be a lot of nailing, sawing, cutting, and hammering in our new life. It is going to take time. But we have confidence that this new life will be a great work of masterpiece because the builder and architect is God!

He provides the building materials, but we cannot distort them with substandard materials that we may have gotten from another source. In the design and assembling of a building, it is conceivable that it takes just one mistake, one missing stud, or substandard material, to cause a building to collapse. It is the same way in the Christian life. If we are building for appearance, we will fall. If we are using inadequate materials, we will fall. If we are not strong, the storms will come and we will be left with a demoralizing situation. We have to be certain that our walk with the Lord is built on Him, the Solid Rock.

Our relationship with Him is built with the materials of prayer, study of the Word and the presence of the Holy Spirit. In turn, He will fortify our relationships in our marriages and with our children, in our friendships, and in the Church. Our children will be trained through the Word of God on a daily basis so that they do not steer away from Him and so that their walk with the Lord will be built to last.

In our ministry, we have to be certain that there is no self-gratification: the glory must be the Lord's and our ministry must be built to last. Our testimony has to be built to last so that we are not tossed around as a reed in the wind. We must live with

If GOD doesn't build the house, the builders only build shacks. Psalms 127:1 (Message)

such conviction that when the testing comes, all will be exposed and He will be pleased because He will find that we built with proper materials, not with a covering of whitewash.

If GOD doesn't build the house, the builders only build shacks. Psalms 127:1 (Message)

# Results of Building with Poor Materials

Psalms 127:1 If GOD doesn't build the house,
the builders only build shacks.

If GOD doesn't build the house, the builders only build shacks. Psalms 127:1 (Message)

~ Page 95 ~

**Chapter 6**

## The Columns

*Revelation 3:12 He who overcomes, I will make him a pillar in the temple of My God, and he will not go out from it anymore; and I will write on him the name of My God, and the name of the city of My God, the new Jerusalem, which comes down out of heaven from My God, and My new name.*

*I*n construction, it is not uncommon to have terms used interchangeably like foundation and footing, or column and pillar. Actually, column and pillar are synonyms of each other and will be designated as such in this book. Pillars can be architectural and ornate in design, but they still provide necessary support to guarantee the stability of a structure. Pillars are designed for a specific need. Some pillars are made of steel, offering a certain amount of foldability in their design. They are interconnected with the sure, deep, and stable foundation that has been established for them and they share a grabbing effect with the reinforcement members to tie together the pillars with the beams or slabs and the load that they are supporting.

If GOD doesn't build the house, the builders only build shacks. Psalms 127:1 (Message)

As I mentioned in previous chapters, reinforcement bars were placed in the foundation or footing and bent upward to allow the concrete columns placed on top of the footing to create a monolithic connection. The solid foundation with the required reinforcement bars will keep the column from subsiding (sinking) into the ground once loaded. Columns can be formed either with a high strength reinforced concrete, masonry, wood, or steel, and they are built onto the previously cured concrete foundation. Usually, if a column is constructed out of steel or wood where a monolithic joint cannot be provided, a base plate will be placed where the column and footing meet in order to share or transfer the load without overstressing the foundation.

There is a definite size and location for each column. The greater the load, the stronger the column needs to be. Columns and pillars are critical to a structurally sound building because not only do they support beams, which in turn support walls and ceilings, but any upper stories are also dependent on their design capacity to sustain the extra load. Pillars in the body are the means of bringing together, supporting, and protecting the different members of a structure.

We hear the saying that certain people are "pillars in their community" and immediately we can picture the impact that person has on the community. All the more reason that Christians should be pillars of the world we live in. We should demonstrate structural soundness in our lives; not perfection, but steadfastness in our purpose. This serves the Lord by proclaiming hope to our communities. Revelation 3:12 portrays an image that we are to be overcomers. It tells us that when a column overcomes any adverse force that acts against it, as in a hurricane,

If GOD doesn't build the house, the builders only build shacks. Psalms 127:1 (Message)

~ Page 97 ~

an earthquake, or tornadic winds, and remains standing, it will become a pillar in the temple of God. It is the storms that prove the pillar will overcome.

As a result of victorious living, we will become pillars in the temple of God, not just for support, but also for permanence. Three parts of an inscription will be made on the pillar. First, because the overcoming life is a testament to God Himself, He will write His own name on that pillar. Second, the City of God, the New Jerusalem that comes down from heaven, will be written as a testimony to the services and work performed for His Church. Lastly, the new name of Christ will be inscribed there: the name which allowed the overcomer to be victorious." Only by Christ's work on the cross, the resurrection, and ascension to heaven could the overcomer succeed to allow the new name to be written on the pillar, the name of our God.

God offers overcomers the reward of being a pillar that will be identified with the name of God. We will become an overcoming testimony to encourage others to resist, to stand fast, and to overcome. The overcoming is not through our own strength, but through our dependence on Jesus Christ, the chief cornerstone. What an honor to be overcomers, able to extend the strength from the foundation to support countless others who follow us! We must not allow the shakeups and tremors of life to cause us to deflect, sway, or buckle. As we sternly focus on God's Word and build godly character, we will become straight and strong pillars, able to help and shelter others. One of the safest places when an earthquake strikes is next to a pillar: a pillar that will stand by our side when temptations and troubles otherwise cause us to fail.

If God doesn't build the house, the builders only build shacks. Psalms 127:1 (Message)

Pillars have an unwavering call to support those that are bearing on them. When a force is passed through an object, the object will be apt to change its form. Often times when we are overloaded, we hide our conditions. Others cannot see what we are going through because we internalize our struggles. A stress may be described as a mobilized internal reaction. Physics tells us that for every action there is an equal and opposite reaction, a reaction which resists any tendency towards deformation. Often, instead of allowing others to minister to us, we are too proud to share the load of the stress that we may be under. There is a tendency to react or overreact within our own strength and capabilities.

Pillars are usually shaped to give an appearance that is pleasing to the eye, but not designed to draw too much attention. Pillars have a role that far exceeds surface facades and architectural appearances. Although they are very strong and usually hold up the rest of the body, they are not easily noticed and in most cases are ignored. Their value comes from an inner strength that cannot be measured. They can withstand the winds of life, the tremors of this world, and they will stand tall when many other properties fall. The pillar will not go out from its position. Be that as it may, some human columns can, and frequently do, try to direct consideration upon themselves rather than on God. These columns become independent, as opposed to putting their reliance on God for strength.

When a designer prepares a set of construction plans, he creates a rectangular grid system that will name each individual pillar and assign it a specific coordinate or location. No two columns have the same inscription, nor the same coordinates.

If GOD doesn't build the house, the builders only build shacks. Psalms 127:1 (Message)

Each has a very specific calling and a specific function. Though their inner makeup may be different, all are accomplishing the same task, and that is to support. Each one of these pillars in the kingdom has the name of God inscribed upon it.

I find it interesting that the passage in Revelation instructs that the pillars are not to go out from it anymore. That means they have an assignment. They are not to go out, bouncing around from ministry to ministry trying to fit into another body that the designer never assigned them to.

They have a certain responsibility of supporting a specific load in a particular place of the ministry.

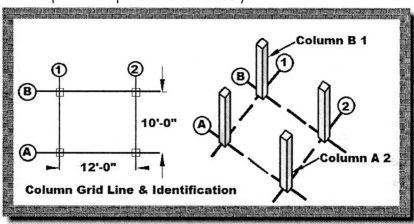

Each has a very specific calling and a specific function.

There are certain loads that only you can support, and certain ministries that only you are capable of performing. Just like my job may not be to admonish a congregation on Sunday morning, likewise it may not be possible for the pastor to reach the people that I work with. We all share in the load of supporting the other members of the body. We should be sensitive and considerate of other members so we do not overstress them or fail to share burdens (loads) with them. Even in the service of the

If God doesn't build the house, the builders only build shacks. Psalms 127:1 (Message)

~ Page 100 ~

Lord, you do not want a newborn Christian handling the load that a stronger, seasoned Christian should handle. Nevertheless, we do not seem to think twice about overloading them, and the end result is a stressed out column that feels all the agonizing stress and strains within it, which eventually will buckle and fail.

Very seldom do you find a building that is supported by just one column, and no column or individual pillar carries the weight that should be evenly distributed. In the world of engineering, the designer will not dare place so great a load on the member that it will eventually fail. The world has a way of loading us down, and even in the church world, there is that tendency. We often struggle to handle our existing stress, yet we continue to pile it on. God has calculated the exact amount of load a pillar (person) can bear, and He does not want us to be a stressed out body or a failed fragmented body.

*1 Corinthians 10:12-13, 12 therefore let him who thinks he stands take heed lest he fall. 13 No temptation has overtaken you except such as is common to man; but God is faithful, who will not allow you to be tempted beyond what you are able, but with the temptation will also make the way of escape, that you may be able to bear it.*

A warning is issued...God hates pride. A single pillar will only support a limited load that is applied directly to it, but through God's omniscience, He made a way that we can survive all that life hurls at us. Nothing is new under the sun in terms of trials and tribulations. Seemingly, there is nothing that can ever happen to you that has not happened to someone else before. It

If GOD doesn't build the house, the builders only build shacks. Psalms 127:1 (Message)

~ Page 101 ~

is for this reason that we should learn from those seasoned pillars that have experienced the storms of life.

It is not God's plan that we succumb to any form of temptation that we cannot bear. If we keep our eyes on Him and trust Him, we can learn from the hard lessons of others. But when we allow ourselves to think we are standing on our own, we subsequently fall. The eternally faithful God has already made provisions for us to have a way of escape. His plan could consist of a redesign to lessen the load imposed: a temporary additional post, additional bracing, rebar, or an additional pillar. Whatever His choice, once we are surrendered, the structure becomes stronger. It is not the plan for a pillar to give up, rupture, or quit, but to recognize it was created for load bearing and full dependence on God.

Some pillars are designed with specific materials according to the proposed loads. For instance, a pillar designed of steel, which has a flexible property, will be able to bend somewhat as loads are applied to the top (axial loads). As the load increases in magnitude, it passes through three states: stable equilibrium, instability, and neutral equilibrium. This is similar to what happens to the body of Christ. Individually, the pillar is initially in stable equilibrium, meaning that there is no static or dynamic movement in the structure when under a certain load. It appears to be able to handle a load, and it is willing to be flexible enough to work with others. It will be a load-bearing member of the church that is ready to serve, provided that its limits of strength are not exceeded. Say a small lateral (side) force is applied between the two ends of the column; it will yield a small lateral deflection.

If God doesn't build the house, the builders only build shacks. Psalms 127:1 (Message)

For some reason, some of us seem to be able to handle a great deal of axial pressure to our lives, and we have a tendency to push it to the limit. If, however, an additional infinitesimal unforeseen sideways load is introduced, it throws us off balance and out of equilibrium and it causes us to go into unstable equilibrium.

Sometimes, though, if the column load of life is gradually increased, stable equilibrium becomes neutral equilibrium. This occurs when a small lateral force produces a bending movement that does not disappear and the column remains in this slightly bent form when the lateral force is removed. Remember the story in Genesis 32 when Jacob, who was a strong pillar, wrestled with an angel all night? At the end of the match, Jacob sustained a dislocated hip that caused him to walk with a limp. This limp is not so much a mark of discipline, but a reminder of an encounter, a mark of equilibrium, which reminded him forever of the seriousness with which he served his God. It was a mark of faith, which he carried to his grave.

One last load to consider is where neutral equilibrium of a column has been reached and some other load is applied that will cause movement or failure. It is the critical or buckling load. Unfortunately, limitations of loads are an area that is not very well guarded by the ministry. According to research studies done by Into Thy Word (4), 1,500 pastors per month leave the ministry because of burnout. Anything, including ministry, which requires us to carry a load beyond what we are able to carry is sin. In the book of Genesis, the second verse of the second chapter begins with, "so on the seventh day He rested from all His work." So you see, even God had to rest.

If GOD doesn't build the house, the builders only build shacks. Psalms 127:1 (Message)

Jesus also recognized His limitations while here on earth, and He took the time to recover. He took to time to fulfill His relationship with His family. Many of us do the same with our work: we work ourselves to the point that we exceed the load that we are able to handle, and then we collapse. We are no different than the solid, rigid, massive chunk of concrete or metal that may initially survive a slight overload but will eventually buckle under the strain.

We should not allow so much of a load to be placed on us to the point that we neglect our families, our health, and our time alone with God. It is the point where we take our watchful eye off of the Lord. At first, the added load may seem insignificant or necessary, but the added weight can cause the entire column to fail, and concurrently other members to fail with it. The state of instability is reached when a slight increase of the column load causes an uncontrollable growing lateral deflection that leads to complete collapse. A column is designed to work in unison with other columns, but because there is a tendency to cover imperfections, the Lord is constantly checking them for flaws and for possible weak areas that can be disastrous to the rest of the body.

Pam and I have been to countries in Europe and the one thing I remember of some of the ancient structures is that there were no roofs, walls, and in some cases no slab, but the columns were still standing tall. God made the columns to stand with His name written on them, to await the return of our Lord.

If God doesn't build the house, the builders only build shacks. Psalms 127:1 (Message)

The tall redwood trees of northern California, a living example of columns that are able to stand tall, survive because the deep-rooted system creates a foundation that covers a large surface area. The tree recognizes its source and it knows how to tap in for nourishment, and it recognizes that its stability is in the contiguous sharing of the load with its adjoining column. When the storms of life come and set additional demanding loads, it knows to reach to God who is faithful. It knows that, when those unexpected loads come, God will provide a way of escape.

In a relative manner, an uncompromising world-changing Christians are the result of a shrouded, interconnected root framework. The Word of God provides the nourishment to grow through love, joy, peace, longsuffering, kindness, goodness, faithfulness, gentleness, and self-control. Against such a taproot the tree is fed, helping it to reach toward the heavens and outward to others. One thing to consider is that these trees are not born as giants; they start from small seeds. We are not born as giants of the faith. Our walk with Christ starts with the small seed of the gospel planted by someone who shares the gospel with us. The seed is planted in soil tilled by the Holy Spirit and watered by God. Our Heavenly Father knows what we need for sustenance, and He provides ways for us to grow through the Holy

If GOD doesn't build the house, the builders only build shacks. Psalms 127:1 (Message)

Spirit, personal prayer, Bible study, fellowship, and church teaching. The growth will result in a large tree with deep roots capable of serving the people it was called to serve, and spreading seeds to germinate new saplings.

*Psalm 1:2-3, ² But his delight is in the law of the Lord, and in His law he meditates day and night. ³ He shall be like a tree planted by the rivers of water that brings forth its fruit in its season, whose leaf also shall not wither; and whatever he does shall prosper.*

As Christians, we should always be looking up toward heaven, trying to discern and fulfill His divine will. Psalm 92 instructs us how the righteous shall flourish like the palm tree.

Let us also consider another tall tree that reaches to the heaven. The leaves of the palm tree provided shelter as they were used for their cooling effect on the roofs. Even today, they are used as a covering for the roofs in some countries. The palm tree has a very acute ability to find water. Its roots go deep to locate water even in dry places. Consider a desert filled with hot sand, and yet the palm tree survives bearing the scorching heat of the sun.

If you have noticed when a hurricane or a strong gust of wind comes, the palm trees along the beach bend almost to 90 degrees or a right angle. The palm tree does not snap. It bends and withstands the forces of the wind. After the storm passes, it will once again stand erect and reach up to the heavens, rejoicing and praising the Lord. Our inner character purified and fed by His

If GOD doesn't build the house, the builders only build shacks. Psalms 127:1 (Message)

~ Page 106 ~

word allows us to be bendable yet strong, with God providing in us an inner strength that will keep us from snapping.

There are so many similarities between these tall trees and pillars or columns of the church. Columns are very tall; they stand erect and are always reaching toward the heavens as if they were looking for the return of our Lord. They are located on a certain place and, regardless of the exterior forces acting upon them, they will never move if they share the load with others. Like the palm tree, they have an internal makeup that allows them to have some flexibilities and yet not snap.

We are to be like the column that stands fast in the temple of our God, supporting others and never departing from our appointed calling, being faithful as an overcomer. We should be like the tall trees always reaching to the heavens, being strong, and overcoming the storms of life that will come to snap us.

If GOD doesn't build the house, the builders only build shacks. Psalms 127:1 (Message)

## Chapter 7

**Deuteronomy 3:5 all these were cities fortified with high walls, gates, and bars, besides a great many unwalled towns.**

𝒜 wall can be an enclosure to a structure that will provide shelter and protection for its inhabitants, or it can be that element that defines the perimeter of an area of ownership and is used to fortify. The word wall comes from Latin *"vallum"* meaning "...an earthen wall or rampart set with pickets." But in Latin, the word vallum is synonymous with the word *"murus"* which means a defensive stonewall that is able to carry a load. In English, we utilize the same word to mean an outside divider or the inward sides of a room, yet this is not all-inclusive. Many languages distinguish between the two. The Spanish language makes a clear distinction between *pared* (a wall) and *muro* (post).

Pursuant to the definitions above, some walls can carry a load, and some provide a buffer against those nagging interferences in our lives, like the noise buffer walls along the side of a highway, that shield us from the barrage of humming from the passing vehicles. Walls can be constructed with various types of materials. There are walls that are constructed with wooden

If GOD doesn't build the house, the builders only build shacks. Psalms 127:1 (Message)

~ Page 108 ~

lodge poles that are plastered with mud. Perhaps they are built like in the Roman times where builders used materials ranging from chalk and sand to Pozzolanic concrete. Unlike the well-graded materials that we spoke about in formulating the mix of concrete, they used debris and broken pottery mixed with mortar in order to fill the wall sections. Generally, the walls that we build can create an atmosphere that is either inviting or deterring.

The Berlin wall was built to divide. It created a separation between groups of people, and it divided them into NATO and Warsaw Pact Zones. The wall was not impenetrable, but it oppressed and isolated people, and it created an incapacitating mental and emotional condition. In like manner, prison walls have been designed and built to create a dejecting environment: unattractive and uninviting.

*Matthew 5:14 ¹⁴ you are the light of the world. A city that is set on a hill cannot be hidden.*

As Christians, in order for us to make an encouraging and a positive difference in this world, we need to become walls that are joyful, inviting, full of life, and not worn, broken or defeated. We need to stand out and be attractive and colorful and have a positive attitude. A great example of an inviting communal wall is Facebook. It is a social networking site used as an electronic "wall" to log the scribbles of friends. It is a wall that has no economic, cultural, racial, or religious limiting boundaries.

Big corporations like McDonalds understand the concept of presenting a welcoming and appealing storefront. Generally, McDonalds can be spotted at a distance because it has an

If GOD doesn't build the house, the builders only build shacks. Psalms 127:1 (Message)

attractive bright color on its walls, golden arches, and a smiling mascot. In our personal lives, we are called to live a different lifestyle than the world: live a lifestyle of purity, of encouragement, and of peace. Our walls need to radiate the joy of the Lord in our lives as proof that we belong to Him.

Walls are built with a purpose, and that is to shelter and protect us. In coastal areas due to destructive and damaging wind storms, construction methods require that protective measures be taken. For instance, J-bolts (steel rod anchor bolts about 10 inches in length and in the shape of a "J") are embedded every 32 inches into the concrete footing or slab. Their purpose is to fasten a 2x4 or 2x6 pre-treated base plate (bottom portion of a framed wall) of a wood

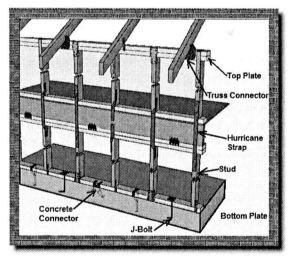

framed wall in order to resist any uplift from the winds, and from tugging the house away from the slab. On the windward side (the side where wind forces push against the house) the winds of a 140-mile per hour hurricane generate approximately 50 pounds per square feet of pressure. That equates to about 32,000 pounds of force for a 40' long by 8' high side of a house, assuming a drag coefficient of 2. This force would equate to three commercial unit fleet trucks like those brown parcel trucks pushing against the house.

If GOD doesn't build the house, the builders only build shacks. Psalms 127:1 (Message)

I do not know that we can place a numeric value on the similar type forces that want to crush us and defeat us, but when we are going through trials in our lives, it seems as if the force of the whole world is pushing against us. These are forces that want to trample us, push us down, and make us give up, forces that push us to the limit. Forces that want to cause us to fail and even uproot us from the very foundation that we should be set on, but the Word says:

**Psalms 30:5, God is our refuge and strength, always ready to help in times of trouble.**

This is a promise that should give us comfort, and we should not fear. He is our refuge and strength even when the winds blow, and the earthquakes come and the mountains crumble into the sea. He is faithful and always there, ever-present in the time of need. On the leeward side (pull of the wind forces) of the building, these forces want to pull us away from His habitation, confuse us with many fears, and separate us from the rest of the body. The Word forewarns us that this is a type of storm that will come into our lives.

**2 Corinthians 4:8-9 we are pressed on every side by troubles, but we are not crushed and broken. We are perplexed, but we do not give up and quit.**

Beloved, let us be anchored down with the revelation and knowledge of the Word of God in unison with other members of the body so that we can resist those unexpected 140-mile-per-

If GOD doesn't build the house, the builders only build shacks. Psalms 127:1 (Message)

hour wind gusts that life blows against us, that would otherwise push us or pull us to a yielding point and eventually blow us away. Perhaps a great shaking will take place that will distress our very foundation and cause it to fail if we allow it. But I say that greater is He that is within me, than any opposing forces that is against me. It is no wonder that the Word warns us that we will perish (be blown or shaken away by outside forces) because of the lack of knowledge of His Word. We need to prepare and build those storm shelters in our hearts and lives with solid walls in expectation of the winds that will surely come. We may be perplexed and troubled, but as long as we have the preparation of the Gospel of Truth, we will stand every trial. These walls that we build in our lives will give us the ability to resist any outside interference or strong forces that come against them.

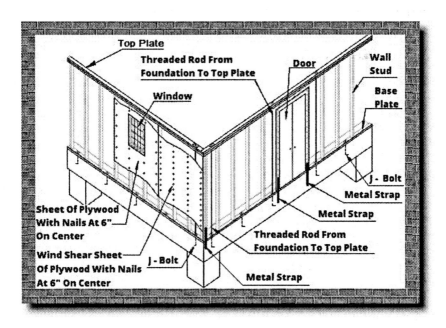

If God doesn't build the house, the builders only build shacks. Psalms 127:1 (Message)

In addition to the J-bolts that are used to anchor us down, strong metal straps are fastened to the corners of the house framing, and at principle openings (like exit doors and windows). These straps represent those mature Christians who have knowledge and experience to handle the storms and quakes of life. I know that this may seem silly, but there is a manufacturer of hurricane straps that is named Simpson. Every time I specify a Simpson Strong Tie like an MAB (Mudsill Anchor Bolt), a metal anchor similar to a J-Bolt, one that is set in a concrete block, poured walls, or slab foundation, I imagine Samson of the Bible holding down the structure. Unfortunately, Samson in his rebellion did the opposite. When he least expected it, he was pulled right out of the foundation that he was supposed to have anchored to. When we get to the place that we think that we are anchored firmly enough and we take our eyes off of God, then we will allow the affairs of this life to uproot us, and as a result, that storm will gouge out our eyes. If we pull ourselves away from the anchoring and strapping that have been provided, a storm can be let loose on us, and it will blow us away.

Threaded rods, made of steel and 5/8 inch in diameter, and are utilized to anchor the structure from the solid concrete footings to the upper side of the top framing plates. This is similar to the anchoring that is required in creating a tie from the very top of our heads to the very bottom of our feet, and it must be made by using the Word of God as our anchor. This is kind of like anchoring heaven and earth. These rods start at the concrete foundation and they project through the very being of our body. They tie to the top plate of the framing, anchoring us from the top of our head to the bottom of our feet, and they are shod with the

If GOD doesn't build the house, the builders only build shacks. Psalms 127:1 (Message)

~ Page 113 ~

preparation of truth. Many protective measures are taken, and that is the reason that we are told that Christ will dwell in our hearts and that our roots will be grounded in love.

The next protective measure for our walls comes once all the 2x4 or 2x6 studs are framed and anchored down. These studs are shielded with sheets of plywood to cover and protect the framing and the interior of the structure. But plywood panels are not just pieces of wood cut from a tree. Plywood sheets are engineered from thin layers or "plies" of wood veneer that are glued together with adjacent layers having their wood grain rotated up to ninety degrees to one another. Similar to the preparation of the foundation, plywood undergoes a process of spreading down glue and then compressing the veneer sheets with an immense force. The final result is an unyielding building material that has undergone stress, pressure, and heat. Likewise, the body of Christ can glue itself and create such a bond that no matter what forces come against us, we can withstand. Alone, one single sheet may be easy to tear, maybe even with our own hands, but a series of plies can withstand a lot of shear forces.

*Ecclesiastes 4:12, though one may be overpowered by another, two can withstand him. And a threefold cord is not quickly broken.*

The proverb used in the verse above is substantiated in the Latin phrase "Vis unita fortior est," which means we are stronger in union. This was the Father's plan from the beginning: the **Trinity**, (Father, Son, and Holy Spirit); **Man**, (Spirit, Soul, and Body); **Precepts** (Faith, Hope, and Love). Where there is a lack of

If GOD doesn't build the house, the builders only build shacks. Psalms 127:1 (Message)

~ Page 114 ~

unity, there will be division leading to ultimate failure. If a house does not contain the properly prepared rigid walls, the enemy, (forces of nature) will cause the building to collapse. The failure will not be seen until it is too late.

One way to envision what this unity may look like within the church body may be with the makeup of different ministries. A wall has several layers that constitute the whole, as in ministries within the body, each with a specific calling. A pastor spends countless hours studying, praying, and preparing his sermon, yet he has a support team that is working in the background. The music department has many members within itself that bond to make it a strong support. The worship pastor may be the most visible part of the wall, but without the musicians, singers, sound engineers, and support staff, the department will be weak and may fail in its purpose. A worship team, composed of different members working together harmoniously, must prepare and practice for its assignment to create a melodic invitation to praise and worship. The kingdom profits when we find our place and our calling. You would not, for example, want me to be the music director, which is not my calling. I took a college course in music theory and, to me, that class was more difficult than Differential Equations. I could not grasp things like half, whole, quarter, sharp, natural, major, diminished, augmented, minor, etc. as it applies to music in my ears. Even the way they write sheet music looked like a bunch of Chinese symbols. If it had been me, I would have written numbers on the music sheet. After all, numbers are universal. I have heard it said that music is mathematical. It may be, but you have to have talent. I guess that is the reason I am an engineer and not a musician.

If GOD doesn't build the house, the builders only build shacks. Psalms 127:1 (Message)

This explains the necessity for those sheets of plywood to be placed at specific locations (generally at the corners that are in the same direction of the prevailing wind) in order to resist shearing forces that come against us and that are generated from the winds. There is no possessiveness of their calling among these sheets; they know that each has to accomplish a specific job in a specific place. One sheet without the assistance of the other will be blown away. All ministries find their place where the specific calling is needed. Just like the plywood sheets, the positioning and amount of nails play a major role in attaching the plywood to the studs. The closer together we are to one another, the greater the force that we will be able to resist when external trouble comes against us.

So to overcome shearing forces from wind, plywood at the corners where wind is more prevalent is fastened at a closer nailing pattern than the other internal sheets. The nail spacing may be reduced from 6 inches center of nail to center of nail down to perhaps 4 inches on the sheets that have been given the assignment of overcoming wind shear. The proper location and construction of those sheets protects us against those shearing forces that are trying to tear us apart.

Like the wall constructed with plywood, a brick wall is built with many members; many bricks carefully glued together with mortar and jointly fit together to form a protective membrane of the house. There are no Lone Rangers. It is a conglomerate of many members (many bricks) all tied together with brick straps and wire, then attached to the wood framing and plywood. We need each other, and when we are precisely joined in unison, we can provide shelter for others that are less fortunate. We can

If GOD doesn't build the house, the builders only build shacks. Psalms 127:1 (Message)

become protective members that will ensure the integrity of those that are not as strong.

*Isaiah 62:6, I have set watchmen on your walls, O Jerusalem; they shall never hold their peace day or night. You who make mention of the Lord, do not keep silent.*

We have to be careful to set watchmen to maintain a watchful eye.  We cannot assume that, because we build with  stronger materials such as concrete blocks or a poured concrete wall, we are safe from harm. We have to be vigilant because we have an enemy that will sneak in to kill steal and destroy.

We cannot just walk away, and assume all is well.  The same measure of care, maintenance, and diligence must be exercised in the anchoring process with these massive structures as in the wooden type structures.  We need to fortify ourselves with the preparation of the Gospel of truth.  If we do not, then we will realize that the forces of this world have come against us.  Satan can attack us like a hurricane gust wind or an unannounced earthquake with a great force that can even take down a massive wall.  We can take protective measures, with all these straps and designs for seismic

If GOD doesn't build the house, the builders only build shacks. Psalms 127:1 (Message)

loads, but we must understand that we wrestle against principalities, against powers, against the rulers of the darkness of this world, and against spiritual wickedness in high places.

We need to learn to be vigilant; to guard every side and put on the whole armor of God, because the enemy will come as a thief in the night. He knows that we live behind walls built with bricks and sticks, blocks or concrete. He knows that we have placed protective measures on the construction, but often times those measures can make us complacent. He will encamp around us and bring down our walls.

There is a story in 1 Samuel 11, where Nahash the Ammonite surrounds the children of Israel at Jabesh Giliad because they got complacent. Instead of seeking God or fighting back, they asked to make a compromise with Nahash. He agreed and set the terms, warning that if they did not find someone to help the inhabitants of Jabesh Giliad, Nahash would gouge out their right eye. There is so much in this story, but the main principle that I want to bring out is that, if we compromise with the world, it will make us ineffective and eventually takes us down. Often times, Satan has been allowed to penetrate our lives, breaching our walls and diminishing our ability to fight back.

*Job 33:4 The Spirit of God has made me, and the breath of the Almighty gives me life.*

A wall provides more than just protection from the elements. A fittingly planned and developed divider is a principal piece of any structure and it has a sprawling effect on its tenants. To build within ourselves a small, confining, and uninviting

If GOD doesn't build the house, the builders only build shacks. Psalms 127:1 (Message)

habitation will cause us to develop a "sick building syndrome," one that will create a sealed off, unhealthy, and depressing environment. Walls ought to be built to be "breathing dividers," on the grounds that, when we do, the breath of the Almighty will give us life. A wall should allow the breath of God to enter in, as He is the Creator of that wall. It is not to be like the Sanhedrin's walls of the temple which allowed only a select few to enter. The walls that we build should be inviting. They should have lots of windows to allow the light of God to enter in and fill our hearts with joy.

The walls should have a door to allow those that need sanctuary to enter. The door is to allow us to have a freedom to move around, to enter in and most importantly to go out and take the gospel to the world. We are not to be secluded with fear as though we are in a prison, waiting on some Nahash to surround us and make us ineffective.

In engineering, the physical process responsible for vapor permeability is called *diffusion*. Diffusion of moisture in air involves movement of water molecules; we, in the church, call it the manifestation of the Holy Spirit. It is He that keeps the right amount of moisture and air in our lives to keep from forming pockets of mold. The walls, however, should not be built just to keep intruders out and to provide us protection, but also to bring those in that are sick with mold infestation, and to allow God's breath to purify, cleanse, and renew them. The walls of the church should be as a clinic with a pulmonary ward, so that people who have very little breath left can be restored. They should be welcomed into the habitation created by the walls **"to allow the Almighty to give them life,"** as Job said.

If GOD doesn't build the house, the builders only build shacks. Psalms 127:1 (Message)

All of us have built different types of walls to keep us separated. Some walls are made of bricks and sticks, some are built of block and mortar, and some are built of more permanent materials. Those walls are easy to build, and the outer layers are visible to the naked eye, but there are other walls that keep us apart. There are walls built between people, families, and even church members that are hard to see. Some of them are kept in secret, disguised by some facade. Some of these walls take a long time, or even a lifetime, to build.

The unseen walls are constructed in our hearts with unwanted materials such as pride. They are laid (one at a time) on blocks of misunderstanding, and we become expert masons that can veneer our walls with colorful bricks of hurt feelings and anger. Sometimes these walls are built on a foundation of religion. Micah tells us that we shall see the downfall of these walls that we build because they are not the walls that the Lord intended for us to build.

Joshua faced walls that seemed impossible to tear down. One of the first parts of the wall that Joshua had to take down was the wall of disobedience of his own people. We, too, have built walls of disobedience and hurt feelings that keep us separated, unable to work together and unable to claim our rightful promise. Joshua knew when he spied out the land that behind these walls were giants who inhabited the Promised Land. We have a tendency to develop our strategies, like sneak attacks. Perhaps the city was either to be taken by assault or by surrounding the city, shutting them off, and starving the people into submission. Another option might have been to weaken the foundation of stonewalls with fire or tunneling. They might simply mound up a

If GOD doesn't build the house, the builders only build shacks. Psalms 127:1 (Message)

mountain of earth to serve as a ramp. This would have been a long process with heavy losses for God's chosen people. Joshua had just experienced the journey in the wilderness that should have taken days but took years because of disobedience to God. The strategy to conquer the city of Jericho was unique, however, because it was laid out by God Himself, and it likely seemed foolish to men.

God chooses the foolish things of this world to confound the wise. God simply told Joshua to have the people march silently around Jericho for six days, and then, after the seventh day, they were to shout and blow the trumpets. Perhaps God caused a combination of the vibration of the marching around the city and the blowing of the trumpets to reach a perfect simple harmonic motion similar to that which brought the Tacoma Narrows Bridge in Washington State, the bridge that swayed back and forth until it collapsed. Whatever the method that God uses, though it may seem foolish, Joshua followed God's instructions to the letter.

At the point when the people did at last yell, the gigantic dividers crumpled in a split second, and Israel won a simple triumph.

As we go through life, we face obstacles as well. Maybe it is a lost cherished person we want the Lord to touch and spare, or a

If GOD doesn't build the house, the builders only build shacks. Psalms 127:1 (Message)

~ Page 121 ~

lost community over which we are burdened. Maybe it is a calling from the Lord that we feel inadequate for, family trouble that tears at our souls, an assailing financial impairment that burdens us to the utmost ranges of our comprehension, or a tormenting sin that dependably alters our life. We must learn not to look upon our obstacles as failures, but as opportunities for the Lord to work in our lives! God is more clearly visible when we are totally out of the picture. In a sense, that is what He did with Israel here. God completely removed them from the equation. The victory at Jericho was all God!

Finally we should learn that faith without works is dead. It is not enough to say, "I believe God." There have to be feet with our faith. We not only have to talk the talk but also walk the walk, and then live in a Godly manner. If we truly believe God, our desire is to obey God. We try to do precisely what God says and keep His statutes. Joshua and the children of Israel carried out the commands of God and, as a result, they were able to capture Jericho.

There are massive walls in our lives that, in our own intellect, seem impossible to take down. But God gave the children of Israel victory over an enemy that was trying to keep them out of the Promised Land. If we have true faith, we are compelled to obey God, and God will tear down the walls that may separate us from Him and each other. He will give us victory over the enemies that we face throughout life. Obedience is the verification that when God guides us to accomplish something, He will provide with no regard to what the spies of our heart tell us. Our confidence is the confirmation to others that we genuinely have faith in Him. We can overcome and triumph in life

If GOD doesn't build the house, the builders only build shacks. Psalms 127:1 (Message)

by trusting in God. The walls that protect our homes from outside environments also provide the sanctuary for the Lord. He has made His dwelling within us, so that in our homes, He is there with us. He wants to dwell close to us, not set aside in some nursing home where we casually visit Him when we find time. Our home, our heart has now become the House of the Lord. These walls shall represent a sanctuary, a sacred place, a consecrated spot, a holy place that cannot be violated by sin; a place of refuge and protection, and a place of shelter.

### Psalm 122

*¹ I was glad when they said to me, "Let us go into the house of the Lord." ² Our feet have been standing within your gates, O Jerusalem!*

*³ Jerusalem is built as a city that is compact together,*
*⁴ Where the tribes go up, the tribes of the Lord, to the Testimony of Israel,*
*To give thanks to the name of the Lord.*
*⁵ For thrones are set there for judgment, the thrones of the house of David. ⁶ Pray for the peace of Jerusalem: "May they prosper who love you.*
*⁷ Peace be within your walls, Prosperity within your palaces."*
*⁸ For the sake of my brethren and companions, I will now say, "Peace be within you."*
*⁹ Because of the house of the Lord our God I will seek your good.*

If God doesn't build the house, the builders only build shacks. Psalms 127:1 (Message)

Chapter 8

## *The Beams*

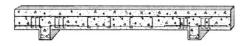

*2 Chronicles 34:10-12, 10 Then they put it in the hand of the foremen who had the oversight of the house of the Lord; and they gave it to the workmen who worked in the house of the Lord, to repair and restore the house. 11 They gave it to the craftsmen and builders to buy hewn stone and timber for beams, and to floor the houses which the kings of Judah had destroyed. 12 And the men did the work faithfully. Their overseers were Jahath and Obadiah the Levites, of the sons of Merari, and Zechariah and Meshullam, of the sons of the Kohathites, to supervise .Others of the Levites, all of whom were skillful with instruments of music.*

*Nehemiah 2:8, And a letter to Asaph the keeper of the king's forest, that he may give me timber to make beams for the gates of the fortress which is by the temple, for the wall of the city and for the house to which I will go. And the king granted them to me because the good hand of my God was on me.*

*O*nce the walls are secured and are accomplishing their purpose, and before the ceiling, second floor, or roof can be added, beams are needed to join the vertical structure together.

If GOD doesn't build the house, the builders only build shacks. Psalms 127:1 (Message)

By definition, a beam is a basic part of the structural members, which generally lies on a level plane between supports (ordinarily columns or walls) and bears contributing loads, and as a rule lie at right angles (90°) to the pillars. Furthermore, the width and depth of the beam are "small" compared with the span (length). Beams are usually very strong and their properties overcome great deflections (bending).

Structural beams come in different sizes and shapes and perform different tasks. They can be simply supported at each end of the beam by two columns, or they may rest upon two walls. There are cantilever beams (used where only one support point can be provided, and the beam overhangs past the support) like a balcony at the exterior of a building. There are continuous beams (beams that are supported by more than one column) that require more supports in their span. These may be used where the load is so great that the bearing capacity (amount of load before failure) has to be assisted by additional columns below it. There are also many others such as lintels, stringers and even girts (for side loads). Just like in the body of Christ, each beam has a specific job to do and no one beam is greater in recognition than the other.

It is imperative that an engineer evaluates the different type of contributing loads so that he can determine the resultant forces acting on the supports of each beam. These can be live, or dynamic, loads (which are loads that can be moved around). Examples of these dynamic loads are furniture, people, and anything that is not fastened down.

The kingdom of God here on earth should be composed of people that are dynamic (live), and should be loads that are

If GOD doesn't build the house, the builders only build shacks. Psalms 127:1 (Message)

~ Page 125 ~

constantly looking for opportunities of growth. As the people of God become static or immobile, there is a possibility of becoming content, stagnant and unfriendly: "me, my four and no more." Jesus commanded us to be dynamic; moving around sharing His love with the entire world.

Beams have a different purpose than the columns, which are designed to stay fixed and not go out from their post. These structural members have a different task: they tie together the columns, or piers, that are steadfast and solid. Like the columns, every member of a church has a specific calling for service. We should not develop a habit of bouncing around from church to church, and event to event. Rather we need to stay attached and faithful to our local body. The beam type members of the kingdom should seek opportunities to minister and places to witness, and they should bring other people (live loads) that will become productive members in the church.

Dynamic type Christians should have a dynamo within them that produces the energy and Holy Boldness to share the gospel of God's love with others. They demonstrate a great influence in this world. However, in the process of a design, any new dynamic load must be accounted for, and it is done through a process of follow-up ministry. This new dynamic load must be placed in the right place and in a specific sustainable ministry. In Structural Engineering, there is a concept in beam design that an **influence line** can be drawn using a unit load (a load that weighs only one unit, it could represent one pound or one thousand pounds).

The influence lines represent the effect of a moving unit

If GOD doesn't build the house, the builders only build shacks. Psalms 127:1 (Message)

load only at a specified point on a member, whereas shear (cutting away like scissors) and moment diagrams (bending) represent the effect of fixed (load that has a specific location, some distance from its end) loads at all points along the member. It is possible to locate the live load (moving load) on the beam so that the maximum value of the reaction, shear, or moment can be determined. The same influence line principle is applicable to intentionally placing a new convert in a designated position. He is a unit load that can be easily influenced or can be an influence to others. He should have a specific place in the body of Christ, for example it is not prudent to place a novice in a place of leadership. His foundation has not been developed or established, and his decisions will affect others.

Another contributing factor is dead loads, or loads that are permanent (nonmoving), including the weight of the beam itself. There is a distinct difference between a dead load and dead weight. A dead load is still an active member, working under tension by stretching and working under compression by being pushed on.

My wife, who is also an engineer, went back to school and obtained a Master's Degree in Counseling so that she could help others navigate through life's struggles. She counsels people with all types of issues or hurts that this life may hurl at them. She guides them along, believing for them that God is the answer, and she points them to Him. It is not an easy job, but she does what God assigned her to do. She is drawn in compassion in such a way that she almost feels their infirmities. I often accuse her of being the world's big sister. She has a great big loving heart and lots of patience. Unlike her, I would be dead weight in that respect. I do

If GOD doesn't build the house, the builders only build shacks. Psalms 127:1 (Message)

not share the similar compassion, patience, or fortitude to listen to other people's problems. It takes time, lots of prayer and tenderness, but because I am a problem solver I expect to see results immediately.

Evangelist and Pastor Jesse Duplantis, in one of his sermon CD's, kids about his style of counseling. He says that when he counsels, he tells clients to: "Repent, do not repeat the offense, and get out of my office." I am certain that he is a kind, gentle, compassionate pastor, but I concur with this philosophically. (Not really, but it is funny.) I am so glad that my wife is a patient and loving woman, with a big, big heart. I have to admit that I am probably her worst case to solve, and it may take her many years of research and counseling before she concedes that I am a challenging lab experiment. But I thank God for her grace and love.

As I said, her tenacity in helping those who appear to be heavy causes is a load that God will take care of. God gives us an inside quality that can bolster dynamic and live loads. Just as a

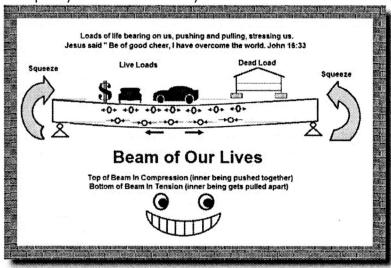

If GOD doesn't build the house, the builders only build shacks. Psalms 127:1 (Message)

proper beam design accounts for all the dead and live loads expected, God gives us His Word to sustain us. In addition to the dead and live loads, there may be unexpected loads due to earthquake, wind, impact, and vibration. Beam design includes the proper span, width-to-depth ratios, material strength, and the specific size and location of the reinforcement bars. All the components must be precise in order to avoid any excessive form of deflection (bending), shear (tearing), fracture (cracking), and ultimately failure.

Some of us may be beams that are bowing and deflecting and are approaching the point of fracture due to loads that life is imposing on us right now. We may be overloaded physically, emotionally, and perhaps relationally. We all have different forms of loads: work, school, finances, family, and health. All these are real loads that burden us, causing us to bend, and in some cases, to reach the point of failure. In our eagerness to serve the Lord, some of us tackle much more than we are able to bear. Other times, without concern of what His plan is, we take on loads that are not part of His design, and we call it self-motivation. Our internal properties may not have the proper width-to-depth ratio or material composition for that particular load. Consequently, we are weakened, and we run out of strength and fail. It is critical that we allow Jesus to show us our optimum load and that we become effective in our individual load bearing capacity. We need to recognize our calling in service and serve according to our own ability.

In the design process, the loads distributed on the beam are those that are applicable to the specific beam. Although the load of an adjoining beam may influence the load and moment

If GOD doesn't build the house, the builders only build shacks. Psalms 127:1 (Message)

~ Page 129 ~

distribution (movement) of the beam being designed, engineers still do a structural analysis on the subject beam and design it for the specific loads. In other words, we are unique and does not need to copy or mimic what another beam may be doing or who it may be supporting. God has different callings, gifts, and ministries for all of us. He has a specific place where we are to serve, and a certain load of the ministry that we are supposed to carry.

The apostle Paul is a good example of this. He was called to preach the gospel to the Gentiles. He did not replicate any other member's spiritual gifts or calling. Paul was unique, and when he received his calling on the road to Damascus, he served God with certainty, and within his gift.

*David says in Psalm 27:4, one thing I have desired of the Lord, that will I seek: That I may dwell in the house of the Lord all the days of my life, to behold the beauty of the Lord, and to inquire in His temple. For in the day of trouble He shall hide me in His pavilion; in the secret place of His tabernacle.*

God may allow the conditions we experience while on earth, whether trials, difficulties, or persecutions, to be used for our better good. Sometimes God may lead us through circumstances to stretch our faith. I look back at the difficulties in my previous years and I count it all joy because it has made me a stronger person. Those experiences have caused me to purge selfish desires. And like King David, I want to live in the house of the Lord all the days of my life. I want to purge all the unnecessary stuff that I have accumulated that can cause me to be burdened,

If GOD doesn't build the house, the builders only build shacks. Psalms 127:1 (Message)

overloaded, and overstressed. I want to purge all the unnecessary things that I have hoarded; things that create a great deal of anxiety when they are broken or missing and that keep me from dwelling in His house.

The previous challenges in our lives may be used to wean us from this world so that we can set our eyes and our affection on the next one. All of us need to find rest for our souls in total surrender to Him rather than in our own intellect. We can carry a great load through Christ who will strengthen us (Phil 4:13) but if we do not abide in Him, we can do nothing (John 15:5). We must allow Him to set our load capacity levels.

When we die, we will not only be in a new house, but we will also have a new habitation; a resurrection body in which our soul will dwell in forever. We should set our eyes and affection to what is coming, to all that the Lord is bringing us into: a new house with a new body with strong beams. This is the reason that we need to stay connected through a network of beams precisely joined together with a supporting group of columns of other believers to help us carry the load.

When designing beams, engineers review diagrams that depict the loads on them and the reactions of the support. These **"free body"** diagrams show us factors such as bending moments, shear, deflection, and reactions at the supports of the beam. In our lives, these diagrams have already been drawn out and the calculations have been made. All we have to do is to read the plans that the Chief Architect has drawn for our habitation, because He knows the plans He has for us.

A simply supported beam is the simplest arrangement of a structure. The beam is supported at two ends. If it is uniformly

If GOD doesn't build the house, the builders only build shacks. Psalms 127:1 (Message)

~ Page 131 ~

loaded, the bending moment is the greatest at the middle and zero at the ends. Therefore, the effect of the maximum moment is at the center. This indicates that the loads of life can be shared by at least two end points or two columns (two people), to resist any failure. The closer we stay to our support group, the greater our capability to carry heavier loads, and the less the deflection. Every beam-supporting column has an understanding and a revelation of its assignment or calling. All are important in the construction of the body.

A member may think that its job is insignificant. It may feel that it does not have a real significant role in the work, or that it does not have any real talent or gifting. It may feel unworthy and remove (Depart)

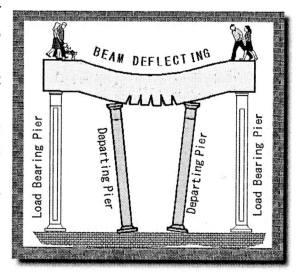

itself from its assigned position. It may think that it will not be needed or missed, but the fact is that as its support is removed, a great deal of stress will be levied on the beam. That beam, in turn, may affect the adjoining columns, and create a negative influence or stress on another member, which creates a negative domino effect that can potentially bring the entire structure down.

If GOD doesn't build the house, the builders only build shacks. Psalms 127:1 (Message)

*Ephesians 2:19 Now, therefore, you are no longer strangers and foreigners, but fellow citizens with the saints and members of the household of God, having been built on the foundation of the Apostles and prophets, Jesus Christ Himself being the chief corner stone, in whom the whole building, being fitted together, grows into a holy temple in the Lord, in whom you also are built together for a dwelling place of God in the Spirit.*

In our lives, we all experience stresses and strains at different times. These outside forces have a direct influence on our adjoining supports. There will be certain failure if we try to walk away or try to handle the loads of life alone. Once we stray, our struggle becomes greater and can bring collapse. The critical thing about contributing loads is that they usually make us go through a fatigue, a tiring period with perhaps an elongation or stretching that is not immediately seen. This stretching usually creates a long-lasting result. For the things we see with the naked eye are temporary, but the things we cannot see are those that creep in as a thief in the night, leaving eternal results. We cannot assume that all is well with our adjoining support, which is the reason that close fellowship is crucial. We are a habitation dwelling together; beams and columns tied together in unison to provide a fit dwelling place that will support every member.

The beams are the extension of Christ's fingers that reach out to His people and tie us all together. To me, it is a beautiful picture of the Lord's crucifixion on two beams. The first beam was a vertical beam column, indicating the relationship between heaven and earth, God and man, always pointing upward where He is constantly watching over us.

If GOD doesn't build the house, the builders only build shacks. Psalms 127:1 (Message)

**Cross**
**Special Support Brace**

The Bible tells us that there is a mediator between God and man, and that is Christ Jesus. He sits at the right hand of the Father, always interceding on our behalf. Now this vertical beam actually becomes a column to support the second beam. This second beam was laid horizontally. Its span points in opposite directions, representing our relationship with each other, our calling to spread the good news and to always support each other. We are to go to the east and proclaim that there is hope; we are to go to the west and proclaim that there is peace; to the north and teach that by one man sin entered the world, but through another, right relationship was restored. We ought to go to the south and show that that there is no condemnation. We are to proclaim those messages in every direction. We need to show that the outstretched arms of Jesus on the beams (the cross) will support the weight of the world. The point of intersection between the two beams became the tie between vertical and horizontal relationships where Jesus gave it all.

There is a song, "If That Isn't Love" that says: "He left the splendor of heaven knowing His destiny was the lonely hill of Golgotha, there to lay his down His life for me." He looked to His side and spoke with compassion to the thief, and He took Him to Paradise. Jesus desires that we see and experience all of our

If GOD doesn't build the house, the builders only build shacks. Psalms 127:1 (Message)

relationships like He does, from the perspective of the cross. I may be a Christian that can only handle a light load, while you may be one that can carry a huge load. But together, in unison with Jesus, we will be able to brace and support each other.

If GOD doesn't build the house, the builders only build shacks. Psalms 127:1 (Message)

Chapter 9

## *Stress and Strain*

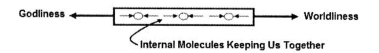

*Psalm 73:25-27,* [25] *whom have I in heaven but you?  And there is none upon earth that I desire besides you.*  [26] *My flesh and my heart fail; But God is the strength of my heart and my portion forever.*

$\mathscr{I}$n engineering, stress is defined as the amount of force that is applied to a certain area.  In materials, there are many names that are given to stress, but stress generally falls into two categories: normal stress and shear stress. Stress in our lives is not abnormal or bad. The important thing is how we deal with it. Stress is a physical condition that reveals internal forces that neighboring particles of a similar material exert on each other. This is similar to the internal forces imposed upon the human heart that can cause a heart attack.  Additionally, another phenomena that affects our lives is strain.  By definition, strain is the measure of the deformation of the material.  This is also similar to the failure of the flesh and is usually noticeable, like a fever blister.

A structural stress examination is performed to guarantee that the structural member's planned use is fulfilled in a certain

If GOD doesn't build the house, the builders only build shacks. Psalms 127:1 (Message)

~ Page 136 ~

load environment. It is critical to try to predict all the ways that our materials can fail. In our lives, once we recognize our weaknesses, we are able to understand God is the strength of our heart and our portion forever.

Did you ever wonder how Jesus was able to handle all the stress that He was under? He may have been God in the flesh, but He still faced grueling demands. Quite often, He had to get away from crowds in order to have personal privacy. He was constantly interrupted with people always wanting something from Him. Individuals repeatedly misconstrued Him, condemned Him, and belittled Him. He had intense anxiety, and great demands on Him that would have caused any of us to fall.

Although Jesus faced immense stress from the people, He knew they were the reason He came. Jesus realized that His strength came from the father above. Because He was part of the Trinity, He possessed all knowledge of the present and future. But His foreknowledge of what He was about to suffer did not make it easier. He agonized to the point that His sweat was like great drops of blood. Jesus knew that He was the Lamb being led to the slaughter and yet he was still willing to sacrifice himself for us.

The pullout strength of a spike similar to what the Romans used to crucify Jesus is about a 5,000 to 6,000 pounds. The weight of His body that was bearing on his hands and feet as He was suspended on the cross was very painful. The Roman nails were designed to shear through the hands, so they placed nails on His feet, allowing Him to overcome the shearing force by pushing upward. Such overcoming upward force, however, was very stressful. Imagine the weight of a small utility truck is about 6,000 thousand pounds. That was the pull-out strength of the spikes

If GOD doesn't build the house, the builders only build shacks. Psalms 127:1 (Message)

~ Page 137 ~

bearing on Jesus' hands and feet. Jesus could have pulled those spikes out of the beams as if they were needles, yet it was not the stress and strain of hanging on the cross that kept Him there. Those Roman nails did not hold Him up on the cross. It was His love for us. He took upon Himself a greater load...the normal and shearing stress of the world.

*Romans 8:18, for I consider the sufferings of this present time are not worth comparing with the glory that is to be revealed to us.*

Stress and strain are a real part of our existence; we face them every day of our lives. They come in the form of many different factors as they are applied directly and indirectly. If a structural element, such as a bolt or a rivet, shears off from a steel member, the member is weakened, and it imposes a shear load on that member and other adjoining members.

As a steel member gets old and is exposed to the elements, it develops an incapacitating disease known as rust. The rust weakens the body as it deteriorates, like a wave of struggles in life that continually beats at us. Yes, there are special paints that cover it, but those are only a temporary fix. The stress is still there and will continue to worsen unless it is completely fixed. Examples of the reality of stress in our lives could be losing your job at Christmas time, which should be a time of rejoicing and celebration rather than a time of inner stress. It could be in the form of a shear force tearing us apart as we face the loss of a loved one. Perhaps a tragic accident, a broken marriage, a failed

If GOD doesn't build the house, the builders only build shacks. Psalms 127:1 (Message)

career, or a friend's betrayal can create such stress. These are such that are common to man.

Jesus and the apostles faced this as betrayal came from Judas, one of their own. He sold Jesus out for 30 pieces of silver. So often, our struggles are unspeakable and we attempt to carry them alone. Our struggles may be unspeakable, but they are no secret to God. He provides a way for us in *Mathew 11:28, Come to me, all you who labor and are heavy laden, and I will give you rest.*

When an engineer designs an enormous structure, there are loads and stresses that have to be taken into consideration. As we discussed previously in the chapters on walls and beams, the loads to analyze are 'dead loads', 'live loads', and 'wind loads.' To reiterate, the dead load is the weight of the structural components itself; the live load is the weight of the daily activities that the structure must carry; and finally, the wind load is the maximum pressure from storms or extreme conditions.

The engineer designs a system of special support 'shear bracings' which make it possible to carry each and every load. When the stresses of life come against us, the Master Builder has accounted for and provided a system of 'cross bracings' to carry us through the storm. The first cross bracing (x-bracing) that Jesus provided for us was a combination of a structural column and a beam that formed the

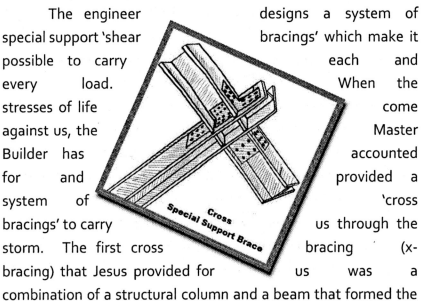

Special Cross Support Brace

If GOD doesn't build the house, the builders only build shacks. Psalms 127:1 (Message)

cross that He hung on. He provided a support beam that makes it possible for us to transfer our own weight (dead load), the weight of life (live load) and the weight of tragedies and trials (wind load). Our Master Builder and Chief Architect, in His mercy and grace, provided us with a 'special support brace.'

In the opening paragraphs of this chapter, stress was described as a physical quantity that shows up through an internal force. In our lives, a lot of stress comes from disguising our internal selves. We try to live a double life by hiding behind a veneer, a fake covering. We create hidden stresses, and the result is a life of insecurity and failure. Insecurity always produces stress in our lives when we feel forced to perform and conform. The only problem is that, when we are hiding behind the mask, we are not accounting for the unknown load which may cause failure when it is finally revealed. Whenever external forces are put on a structure, inward reactions are created and battle to hold the structure together. Once engineers know what loads will be acting on a structure, they calculate the resulting internal stresses, and design each structural member (individual pieces of the structure) so it is strong enough to carry the loads without any chance of failure.

Stresses in the form of tension can occur when two pulling forces directly oppose each other. It is the stretch, the tension that attempts to pull it apart, that will yield a failure (for example, pulling on a rope). Imagine being the rope with two opposite forces pulling on you. On the one side, you have the world, tugging, enticing, and bombarding you with uncontrollable thoughts. On the other side, you have righteousness and desire to serve God completely.

If GOD doesn't build the house, the builders only build shacks. Psalms 127:1 (Message)

~ Page 140 ~

The result of the opposing forces is that the rope experiences a great deal of internal stress. This stress is your inner being, the inside molecules that are pulling back trying to keep from being ripped apart.

The truth is that we are not strong enough within ourselves. An outer force is necessary to help us with the struggles of this tug of war that is occurring within us. The only way that we can overcome these stresses is by studying the Word and finding out what the Lord instructs us to do, and this will be enlightened by the Holy Spirit as we go to the Lord in prayer. No wonder the Bible tells us that we are to turn to Him and He will give us rest. He is the equalizer. He will bring things to balance so that, when we are weak, He is strong. We all face stress at one time or another and in one form or another, but we have Jesus there to fill the gap. He is my refuge, my strong tower and strength.

I was on a mission trip and, as was customary, we took a day off for rest and relaxation at the end of the week. We embarked on a small boat that traversed calm and peaceful waters to a small island. The sun was out, without a cloud in the sky, and the water was like a sheet of glass. We arrived at the island, and it was as majestic as heaven. It was plush with coconut trees, mango trees, all type of fruit trees and palm trees that welcomed our arrival at the beach. It was beautiful, and it surely felt like paradise. There were no worries, no traffic, no store lines, no clocks, and no bills to pay. It was total serenity.

I remember exploring the island with a friend and taking pictures of all the wild life and exotic flowers. Time flew quickly for this peaceful time and we had to return. Again, we embarked

If GOD doesn't build the house, the builders only build shacks. Psalms 127:1 (Message)

on the small boat, and the sea was as still as before: calm and beautiful. Suddenly, out of nowhere, clouds appeared; prevailing winds arose. The glass-like waters turned on us with a tormenting vengeance. The waves seemed like they were way over our heads, taller than the tallest person on the boat. I checked, double checked, and triple checked to be certain that my life preserver was secured tightly.

I reached in my backpack and confirmed that my little pocketknife was in there. I knew that if I was thrown overboard, I would have to fight sharks with my little pocketknife. I looked back to the boat captain, and he was standing there with a smile on his face. Suddenly the boat engine ran out of gas. The captain was still smiling while he and his assistant changed out the gas tanks. I recall that my fears turned into anger. I remember thinking, "You moron. Why did you not switch out the gas tanks before we set out to return?" The captain was still smiling.

I understood why the disciples were anxious when the storm arose and, like the captain on my boat who had no worries, Jesus napped without worries. Captain we are about to be capsized and you do not care? Actually what the captain was doing was keeping his temperament under control, so that the passengers did not lose confidence in him. When a giant wave was about to strike the boat, the captain started the boat and out-paced the wave. Needless to say, we made it to land and the Lord spared me so I could write this book. Not really. But this was a real time of stress and anxiety.

Jesus himself had to turn to the father in prayer in those agonizing moments when He knew that the very people that He

If GOD doesn't build the house, the builders only build shacks. Psalms 127:1 (Message)

loved and came for were about to take His life. He prayed earnestly to the father above.

Stress and strain are physical properties in the material world of structures as well as in our lives. The thing to do is to be certain that we have overcoming forces. When the stresses of life seem to want to tear us apart, we need to be equipped with the Word of God, proclaiming his peace. We need to exercise and equip ourselves with the preparation of the Gospel of Truth. It is not positive confession or behavior modification; these are by-products as we embrace God.

If God doesn't build the house, the builders only build shacks. Psalms 127:1 (Message)

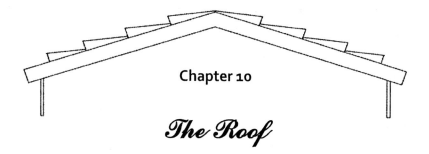

Chapter 10

*The Roof*

**Genesis 1:6 – 7,** *⁶ Then God Said, "Let there be a firmament in the midst of the waters, and let it divide the waters from the waters." ⁷ Thus God made the firmament, and divided the waters which were under the firmament from the waters which were above the firmament; and it was so.*

*A* roof is the covering on the uppermost part of a structure, and it provides shelter and protection from the elements, particularly rain, heat, wind, and sunlight. The dictionary defines the word roof as the exterior top covering or surface and its' supporting assemblies on the top of a structure. The construction of the roof is dependent upon the purpose of the building. God's plan of creation was for man to have a cover, a roof of protection over his head.

Even in the design of the planet earth that we live in, God made provisions for a covering, or a roof if you please, over our heads. The earth's atmospheres are composed of four layers and are based on temperature. The outer-most layer is called the thermosphere, and this layer protects us from the constant bombardment of the sun's rays. Its molecules absorb a great deal of energy from the sun. The next layer is the mesosphere, a cold

If GOD doesn't build the house, the builders only build shacks. Psalms 127:1 (Message)

~ Page 144 ~

layer that is impenetrable to the point that it will slow down and burn up meteors as they hurl toward our surface. The stratosphere is the next layer, which is about 22 miles deep and warmer on the top than at the bottom.

This is the layer that houses the ozone layer that protects us from the sun's ultraviolet rays. The last layer, the troposphere, is the layer that is closest to the earth's surface. This layer is about 6 to 10 miles thick and it contains 75% of the atmospheric mass. So you can see that the Lord, in His mercy and care, provided us with a roof over our heads to protect us from the sun's flares and ultraviolet rays; a layer thick enough to protect us from meteors

If GOD doesn't build the house, the builders only build shacks. Psalms 127:1 (Message)

and to house the gases needed for us to survive. The firmament is the earthly cover acting like a dome or roof around our atmosphere, keeping the waters in their pre-designed places, this is the hydrologic cycle that includes the clouds, evaporation, and condensation.

Where we live, the city lights are not very bright and they do not overpower the natural lights of the stars in the heavens. I really enjoy walking my Golden-Doodle dog, because I am able to see the vast number of stars covering the sky. I always wonder why there are so many stars. I try to count them knowing it is an impossible task to finish. Marveling at the limitlessness, I also ponder that a God who created the firmament and placed all those stars in their appointed places is a God who took the time to build and create me.

*Psalm 8:1-4, ¹ O Lord, our Lord, how excellent is Your name in all the earth, who have set Your glory above the heavens! ² Out of the mouth of babes and nursing infants You have ordained strength, because of Your enemies, that You may silence the enemy and the avenger. ³ When I consider Your heavens, the work of Your fingers, the moon and the stars, which You have ordained, ⁴ what is man that You are mindful of him, and the son of man that You visit him?*

We are so blessed to live by an incredibly beautiful Gulf Coast where the beaches are covered with sand that is as fine and white as sugar. My wife loves to pray there, as she appreciates its beauty. She is overwhelmed with the roaring of the waves breaking on the shore, and she feels secure, as if she was under

If GOD doesn't build the house, the builders only build shacks. Psalms 127:1 (Message)

the roof (firmament) of her Heavenly Father. There is, in comparison, the knowledge that the grandeur of the gulf can be a place of serenity in one moment, but in another can produce a storm that will alter our perpetuity. It is the covering of God that will reassure and protect us wherever we are, for He is our refuge and strength.

*Isaiah 25:4, you have been a refuge for the poor, a refuge for the needy in their distress, a shelter from the storm.*

As the dictionary defines roof, it is the exterior top covering or surface and it's supporting structures on the top of a building. We find that the physical construction of a roof consists of two parts: the supporting structure and its outer skin. Both are equally important. The supporting structure of a roof usually consists of beams or trusses that are long and strong, built with rigid materials such as timber, steel, or concrete beams

The outer skin of the roof, also known as underlayment and covering, is a waterproof system constructed on top of the structural roof. It is a system, usually called built-up felt roofing, which bonds two or more layers (typically three) commonly bedded with hot bitumen (tar). Likewise, the body of Christ needs a layering system so that one covers the other and the bond between each is much stronger. It is through this process that the church can withstand the wind and hail storms of this world. We must also understand that this bonding agent will be applied at extremely high temperature, but as it cools down it adheres together and the result is an impenetrable covering. Likewise in

If God doesn't build the house, the builders only build shacks. Psalms 127:1 (Message)

~ Page 147 ~

our lives, when we go through trials that test our faith, the heat is turned on, but the end result produces a covering that endures.

In some foreign lands, flat roofs are common mainly because of the arid climate; water drainage is secondary so there is not a concern about any ponding or pooling of water. These flat roofs provide an ideal surface for sleeping, bathing, drying food or textiles, gardening, enjoying the cool of the evening, talking to one another, and admiring the stars. It is interesting to see how the covering (roof) is used for many purposes besides keeping the elements out.

The importance of a physical roof correlates to the spiritual covering. There are three major Hebrew words which have been interpreted as "covering." The first is **"sâkak' (הָכַשׂ)"** and is translated to mean cover or placing a hedge around. Think of this word as protection or defense. In other words, men can protect themselves by joining together, fortifying their position, or hedging themselves in such a way that the enemy cannot see or reach them. The sâkak' covering is what that the devil could not penetrate to harm Job. God places a sâkak' covering over our lives that allows our possessions to increase in the land.

The second Hebrew word is **"kasah (כָּסָה)."** The primary meaning of this word is to cover for secrecy. It also means to cover over or conceal. We are instructed that, with love, sin will be covered and concealed.

*1 Peter 4:8, And above all things have fervent love for one another, for "love will cover a multitude of sins."*

If God doesn't build the house, the builders only build shacks. Psalms 127:1 (Message)

~ Page 148 ~

This is not to imply that sin is hidden and not dealt with, but rather that the church body does not magnify and spread its faults. We are to love one another because, if we do not, then we do not know that God is love. This roof covering allows for sin accountability and repentance. This is the covered place where we can do as James instructs us: confess our faults one to another and pray one for another. This does not mean that we reveal all our shortcomings to everyone in the congregation, but rather that we find someone that we can confide in and who can help us and in "kasah" take it to the throne room of heaven. The third Hebrew word for covering is the one that encompasses all of God's plan for man through Jesus..."kaphar(כָּפַר)." It simply means to make atonement. As opposed to kasah, which is defined as covering something over, kaphar means to completely wipe it out, annul it, and make it non- existent. The kasah will cover us with various bituminous substances, as mentioned above in the sealing of the roof. This kaphar shield is the Blood of Jesus on our lives. The church or the body of Christ is the place of covering (roof) where we can come and receive the propitiation for our sins. All that is required of us is to be willing to go to the throne room of heaven and ask Jesus for the propitiation of our sins. Not just to kasha, to conceal it, but to allow Jesus to kaphar, to wipe out our sins, and set them as far as the east is from the west.

Let us consider a couple of examples of how a physical roof can destroy an enemy or open the heart to sin.

*Judges 16: 25-30, ²⁵ so it happened, when their hearts were merry, that they said, "Call for Samson, that he may perform for us." So they called for Samson from the prison, and*

If GOD doesn't build the house, the builders only build shacks. Psalms 127:1 (Message)

*he performed for them. And they stationed him between the pillars. ²⁶ Then Samson said to the lad who held him by the hand, "Let me feel the pillars which support the temple, so that I can lean on them." ²⁷ Now the temple was full of men and women. All the lords of the Philistines were there—about three thousand men and women on the roof watching while Samson performed.*

*²⁸ Then Samson called to the Lord, saying, "O Lord God, remember me, I pray! Strengthen me, I pray, just this once, O God that I may with one blow take vengeance on the Philistines for my two eyes!" ²⁹ And Samson took hold of the two middle pillars which supported the temple, and he braced himself against them, one on his right and the other on his left. ³⁰ Then Samson said, "Let me die with the Philistines!"*

*And he pushed with all his might, and the temple fell on the lords and all the people who were in it. So the dead that he killed at his death were more than he had killed in his life.*

Samson fell in love with a Philistine woman named Delilah, a woman filled with treachery. The Philistines offered her a great deal of silver if she could discover the secret to Samson's strength. Although Samson was set apart, and was under the covering of God, he chose to disobey and disavow it. Delilah set out to capture the secret to Samson's strength. In conjunction with her conspirators and Samson's enemies, she devised a way to persuade him to give her the answer for the riddles that he had posed to them. Using all the trickery and the "hide-and-seek" game, Samson played along with the game of constant pursuit, and eventually ended up with his secret being found. Delilah

If GOD doesn't build the house, the builders only build shacks. Psalms 127:1 (Message)

received her reward: the secret. Samson was clipped of his long hair and the Lord also removed His covering from him.

What Samson never saw when he had two good eyes was that his strength came from the Father above. It was not until the Philistines apprehended him, plucked out his eyes, and cast him into prison that he was able to recognize that the Lord was his roof and covering. Time passed, his hair grew back, and the Philistines were worshiping and making sacrifices to their pagan god Dagon. They brought Samson out to make a spectacle of him and mock his God. Little did they know that in Galatians 6, the Bible tells us that we are not to be deceived for God is not mocked. Perhaps they thought that they had conquered Samson and, worse yet, his God. In the end, though, they were the ones who were sacrificed.

Samson prayed one last time for the restoration of the strength that he now realized came from God, knowing the plan he had would cost him his own life. It seems certain to me that the structure above Samson's head was an interconnection of beams and columns holding not only the roof, but also the Philistines that were above and over Him. God allowed Samson to put his hands at the place of the strongest focal point where the

If GOD doesn't build the house, the builders only build shacks. Psalms 127:1 (Message)

structure rested. God answered his prayer and Samson pushed over two mighty pillars of the temple, causing the roof to collapse. The collapse killed 3,000 Philistines, and Samson himself was killed as well. In a contest between being under the covering of God, or under the covering of man, God will always triumph.

Samson showed that leaving the covering and the protection of God cost him his life. We, too, have a roof of protection over our heads, and we must understand that God did not design the roof so we could hide the majesty of the stars above, but so that we can see them through the glory of His eyes, and in His time. While Samson was able to bring retribution to those against God, we will see how David lived his entire life personally suffering for leaving God's covering. This is another example of leaving God's covering that resulted from pride.

*2 Samuel 11:1-5 [1] It happened in the spring of the year, at the time when kings go out to battle, that David sent Joab and his servants with him, and all Israel; and they destroyed the people of Ammon and besieged Rabbah. But David remained at Jerusalem. [2] Then it happened one evening that David arose from his bed and walked on the roof of the king's house. And from the roof he saw a woman bathing, and the woman was very beautiful to behold. [3] So David sent and inquired about the woman. And someone said, "Is this not Bathsheba, the daughter of Eliam, the wife of Uriah the Hittite?"*

*[4] Then David sent messengers, and took her; and she came to him, and he lay with her, for she was cleansed from her impurity; and she returned to her house.*

If GOD doesn't build the house, the builders only build shacks. Psalms 127:1 (Message)

~ Page 152 ~

*5 And the woman conceived; so she sent and told David, and said, "I am with child."*

It was protocol for the king to be with his men, and it was the spring of the year; the time when kings went out to fight. There is always an appointed time and task that we are to follow. If, however, we choose our own doing, then we get out from under God's covering. King David was to be out in the battlefield fighting, but King David was not where he should have been. Instead, we find him sending Joab and his servants to go out to fight without him. Providentially, they won the battle. King David may have felt that, because he was the king, he could summon others to do his work. He may have felt that he was above the laws and commands of the Lord because he was king. David may have been king, but he was not the king of his life, and we are not the kings of ours. Jesus is the King of Kings and Lord of our lives. Our lives are not our own, and we are subject to His covering.

David finds himself in a place where he left the covering of God. He may have believed that, as king, he did not need to risk death in battle. Whatever his reason, he stepped out on the rooftop trying to go above the covering by himself, forsaking accountability to others around him.

When we get away from the covering of our God, our natural instincts will engage and cause us to see with our natural eyes, leading us to stumble. When David stepped out on that roof, away from the covering of God, he saw Bathsheba bathing and immediately began plotting, which led him to sin, to failure. At first he rebelled openly. It is noted in the scripture that he openly inquired about the woman, and then he even sent others

If GOD doesn't build the house, the builders only build shacks. Psalms 127:1 (Message)

~ Page 153 ~

to do his dirty work. He sent messengers and he took her. Then the devious plot thickened when he covered one sin with another, including murder.

The Bible tells us that there is a way that seems right unto a man, but the end will bring us destruction. One thing that we need to understand is that both God and men cover sin. God does so by the shed blood and glorious grace of Jesus. Man does so by deceit and hypocrisy. Romans 3:23, *for all have sinned and fall short of the glory of God.* Yet different men choose different ways to deal with the aggravation of their failures. The choice is not whether to deal with sin or not, but whether to deal with it wisely or foolishly; to deal with it either righteously or wickedly.

Yes, the purpose of the roof is to cover and protect the rest of the body, but it also covers the head. Pastors need protection: an accountability partner, other pastors, and, of course, the congregation, to cover them and help them when repairs are needed. In order to make repairs on the roof, we may have to apply a covering agent, but not just any agent will do. It has to have the right consistency and viscosity of the bituminous tar that we choose to apply. It is not just the blood of any animal, it has to be the blood that Jesus shed for our sins.

I have traveled abroad to Rome, France and England, and one of my favorite places to visit in those countries is the cathedral-style church. I look up toward the heaven and see the massive wooden beams, rafters, tongue-and-groove planks, and the support beams below the decking. It is amazing to think of all the years these roofs have endured punishment from the elements, and of all the people who have walked under the covering and sheltering of them.

If God doesn't build the house, the builders only build shacks. Psalms 127:1 (Message)

My wife and I visited the Cathedral in Washington DC and, during that time, they were making repairs to the roof system because of a small earthquake that had occurred and caused some damage. As massive as those beams and structural components are, a small leak penetrated and created complications for the integrity of the entire building. As the rain came, naturally, it created havoc on the massive trusses and, eventually, in the inner parts of the building. Just because we have been in church all of our lives, we have memorized scriptures, we have become pillars of the church, does not mean that a small life earthquake will not produce leaks. It does not mean that the covering has not weakened, exposing our spirit to the elements, which in turn, produces rot to our support system creating a weakness in our lives and affecting others around us. Most of the time, these leaks do not show up as a gush of water or a torrential storm, but they creep in one drop at a time. That is exactly what sin does in our lives. It creeps in one little white lie at a time and then it becomes a destructive disaster.

David experienced this when he stepped out on the roof. It may have been another ordinary day in his life, but when he fell into sin, his life became a torrential storm of deceptions and cover-ups that he could not stop. I relate sin to a sluice tube in a water park: once you start downhill and it gains momentum, it becomes frictionless and very difficult to stop. This is why we need the covering of someone like the prophet Nathan who called David out and pointed out his immorality.

We can get so callused and stubborn that the Holy Spirit will allow us to slide down that sluice tube and end up at the bottom of the pond of water, desperate and drowning till we cry

If GOD doesn't build the house, the builders only build shacks. Psalms 127:1 (Message)

~ Page 155 ~

out for help. Then God will send us a life saver and bring us back under the covering through the atonement of Jesus. The only way of escape is to turn to God, ask for forgiveness, and avoid the sluice tube of sin. A small leak in any roof of any structure will eventually lead to a major repair project. When sin is revealed, the course of action determines the future. One person may cover his sins and will not prosper; the other person confesses and finds mercy. Sooner or later we will have to face the consequences of our offense.

When the Lord allows me the opportunity to build another house for myself, I want to include a portion of the roof where I can step out and marvel at the works of His hand. When I consider the heavens and the earth, the moon and the stars, that there is an exact gravitational attraction between each of them maintained by God, that God measure the universe with the span of His hand, and holds the waters of the universe in the hollow of His hand, who am I that God is mindful of me? I am His child, and He knows me by name. That is who I am. Like Job, He placed a covering, a roof over and around me, and a hedge of protection to shelter me. It is up to me to stay under His roof, the roof of protection, the roof of correction, and the roof of direction for my life. I want to briefly share a different type of experience about a roof that the Bible speaks about that is found in the book of Mark.

*Mark 2:2-5, ² immediately many gathered together, so that there was no longer room to receive them, not even near the door. And He preached the word to them. ³ Then they came to Him, bringing a paralytic who was carried by four men. ⁴ And when they could not come near Him because of the crowd, they*

If God doesn't build the house, the builders only build shacks. Psalms 127:1 (Message)

~ Page 156 ~

*uncovered the roof where He was. So when they had broken through, they let down the bed on which the paralytic was lying. 5 When Jesus saw their faith, He said to the paralytic, "Son, your sins are forgiven you."*

Jesus had been out preaching, teaching, and healing around the city of Capernaum. He had been away from the four walls and roof covering proclaiming hope. The house where he was staying was full of people who had heard Him preach and teach and had seen Him heal. There were some friends who had probably seen Jesus heal other people that same day, and they thought that perhaps Jesus could heal their paralyzed friend as well. These friends were resourceful and persistent. One thing that stood out to me is that this paralytic man was one of four children, but the Bible does not make reference to any of his siblings taking an active part in taking the paralytic to receive healing from Jesus. I have to believe that the friends represented the same affection and compassion that Jesus showed, that He is a friend that sticks closer than a brother. They were deliberate, determined, and faithful, and willing to take the risk of being chastised by the elders in order to get their paralytic friend in front of Jesus. They did not let a crowd hinder

If GOD doesn't build the house, the builders only build shacks. Psalms 127:1 (Message)

them from doing so. The friends took their paralyzed friend up the stairways to the roof, took their tools along with them, and dug a hole in that dry clay roof. This is one of the many stories where Jesus emphasized the power of faith.

It was not just the healed man who had faith, but also his friends. The four friends were determined that they would pierce through the roof that was built to keep the elements out, the place of covering overhead. Jesus perceived in His spirit that the religious scribes might be more concerned about the vandalism rather  than the compassion they demonstrated in bringing their friend to Jesus. Jesus illustrated that He had power on earth to forgive sins, and He commanded the paralytic to arise, take up his bed, and walk to his own house.

There were five characters in this story: the friends, the paralyzed man, Jesus, the religious scribes and also the roof. The friends were determined; they were doers, men of action. These men had purpose, and a tile and clay roof and some beams were not going to deter them from helping their friend receive a blessing. The scribes simply want to bring chastisement and condemnation. But there is no condemnation for those who are in Christ. I imagine the paralyzed man being an encourager to the

If GOD doesn't build the house, the builders only build shacks. Psalms 127:1 (Message)

~ Page 158 ~

other four. He had nothing to lose, and he was not a self-pitying man. I did not find any reference in the scripture to him instituting this plan to go through the roof or to him commanding the other four to take him to the healer.

Jesus is the fourth character found in this story. In the previous chapter in The Bible, we find Him where "He was willing" to cleanse a leper. We find Him with a compassionate centurion requesting that his servant be healed, and Jesus said, "I will come and heal him." The centurion felt that he was not worthy that Jesus should come under his roof, so Jesus simply spoke the word that the servant be healed. Jesus went into Peter's house under his roof and healed Peter's mother in law. He touched her and the fever that she had left her. We find Him teaching us lessons in which discipleship is costly.

We have to be willing to step out from under the roof that has us covered. He tells us that the foxes have holes and the birds of the air have nests, but that the son of man has nowhere to lay his head down. The roof provides us with some shelter and some protection, but the only sure place that we have is in Him, not under a covering of a roof made by the hands of man. After all, He is the Son of God, and even the winds and demons are subject to Him.

The last character is the roof. The roofs that we build today should be durable and strong but they need to be penetrable to allow the Holy Spirit to enter in. I want to get to a point where my prayers are so powerful that all of heaven hears them; fervent prayers that avail much. I want them to move heaven to the point that God will dispatch the answer and it will come through all the layers of the atmosphere and penetrate

If GOD doesn't build the house, the builders only build shacks. Psalms 127:1 (Message)

through the roof that I have built. I want to be in a church that is solid enough to provide a covering of protection over my family and me, but such that our prayers will penetrate through and reach heaven.

There is one important thing that I almost left off, and that is how the roofs are built when they are many stories high. There are many components of the roof, like the beams, planks, metal roofing, and in some cases glass. They have to be elevated to high levels, in some cases over 100 feet high. One way that this is done is by erecting a crane using a hydraulic ram system. One important thing is that before you can go up, you must go down first. Before you can be elevated to a higher level by God, you have to go down on your knees and humble yourself before him. Before the crane can go up, in some cases a massive concrete base at the bottom, usually many feet below the natural ground, must be constructed in order to tie the crane to it. This has to be a sure foundation with a slot that the lower portion of the tower crane can be placed on and which it will rest upon.

The next thing is that the tower crane cannot do is to stand up on its own. It needs the cooperation from another crane to

If GOD doesn't build the house, the builders only build shacks. Psalms 127:1 (Message)

~ Page 160 ~

raise up the lower vertical base of the crane, and to also set the horizontal member jib (this is the boom that swings around). We need others to help us when we cannot accomplish the task by ourselves. We need men like Aaron and Hur who raised Moses' arms in an effort to win their battle. As Joshua was out in the battlefield, Moses was lifting him up in prayer.

There is methodology and order in the process; we cannot build the roof first and then work down. The tower crane grows as we ought to grow. It is progressive as we should be progressive. There are no such things as spiritual geniuses. Even the apostle Paul who wrote the majority of the books in the New Testament had to go through a training process. The tower crane using this hydraulic ram system takes in a new crane segment and slides it in to its body, and keeps them aligned and simultaneously pushes upward toward the heavens.

One thing to note is that the crane needs the assistance of men to anchor each segment. Even though it is progressing upward, it still needs the participation of others. It takes work, and it takes time. Construction in our lives is by no means instant. The sanctification process takes time. In order to construct the roof, all the other support members have to be in place as they attribute their progress to the Lord.

If God doesn't build the house, the builders only build shacks. Psalms 127:1 (Message)

Chapter 11

# The Construction
# Project Manager

**2 Chronicles 34:10 then they entrusted it to the men appointed to supervise the work on the LORD's temple. These men paid the workers who repaired and restored the temple.**

$\mathcal{T}$he person responsible for overseeing the construction

of a structure is the project manager. The project manager is accountable for the implementation of the strategic plan that is outlined on the construction plans by the project architect or engineer. He will manage the construction to provide a top-quality product. Ultimately, he will deliver the project according to the standards mandated by the designers and it is his responsibility to deliver it on schedule. He manages all subcontractors and vendors involved in the construction, and he must be knowledgeable of all the aspects of construction and committed to delivering an exceptional project on time and on budget. The project manager is directly responsible for all municipal activities concerning the

If God doesn't build the house, the builders only build shacks. Psalms 127:1 (Message)

construction of the building, including obtaining all permits, scheduling regular inspections as required, and maintaining all regulatory activities. He will often negotiate contracts with architects, vendors, sub-contractors and other workers. As a project progresses, project managers monitor worker productivity and compliance with building and safety codes.

Since he must guarantee that an undertaking is finished, administrators must resolve issues that emerge because of severe climate, crises or different issues that may bring about postponements. The project manager takes a lead role to be certain that all the different disciplines have all the resources that are needed to complete the task.

There is an eagerness to see the project come to completion, so the project manager is careful to remember he is not a taskmaster or a tyrant, lording over those under his charge, but he is an example to all those under him. Often times, in the construction process, there are situations where it seems nothing is going right. Without proper management, the project is in a constant state of disarray. When it has been raining for days, the materials are not delivered on time, and the subcontractors are out of sequence and in a state of confusion, circumstances can eventually shut down a project.

There is no substitute for an experienced and knowledgeable construction project manager. Project managers ensure that all parties are treated fairly. Churches building large complexes, for example, need the knowable advantage of construction project managers to assist in the effort of maximizing and protecting their investment. Even for smaller churches, the benefit of using a construction project manager

If GOD doesn't build the house, the builders only build shacks. Psalms 127:1 (Message)

could be substantial in sheltering allocated investments. Construction management can result in an exceptional finished building project below cost. Project managers help the building process go more smoothly for construction projects. Too often, however, in an effort to cut expenses, project managers are eliminated, and yet they are the professionals that can represent the best interest of the client in a professional manner.

*1 Peter 5:2-4,  ² Shepherd the flock of God which is among you, serving as overseers, not by compulsion but willingly, not for dishonest gain but eagerly; ³ nor as being lords over those entrusted to you, but being examples to the flock; ⁴ and when the Chief Shepherd appears, you will receive the crown of glory that does not fade away.*

One of Jesus' favorite metaphors for spiritual leadership was that of a shepherd, a person who tends God's flock. A shepherd leads the flock as he is led by God. He feeds them the heavenly manna that is found in the Word, nurtures them, corrects them, comforts those that are tired and weary, and protects His flock. These are the responsibilities that belong to every church project manager: the pastor.

From Latin, the word pastor, *pascere*, is defined as shepherd, as one who feeds. Jesus even went further to expound on the responsibilities one has as a project manager, a shepherd, a pastor. The project manager has to be flexible with all the challenges that confront him, and must be willing to adjust to fit the need. Over and over again, we have to adjust our lives to meet

If GOD doesn't build the house, the builders only build shacks. Psalms 127:1 (Message)

~ Page 164 ~

the changes and roadblocks inhibiting us from moving forward. These changes, however, need to follow God's direction.

Consider Noah, a man that lived in the desert, who perhaps may never have seen the ocean. He suddenly found himself commanded by God to build an ark. For Noah, it was a new direction. With no maritime experience, engineering background, nor ship building architectural knowledge, he was able to manage the construction of the ark. With God's help, he became not only a construction project manager but also a project manager who ensured that all the animals were brought to the ark, and that the animals and humans all survived as God had instructed.

Another example is Moses, who was raised in Pharaoh's palace with all its luxury and comfort. Even with this lifestyle, Moses made a deliberate choice to suffer for his people. After killing an Egyptian who was beating one of the Israelites, Moses fled into the desert. While the desert training was necessary for his upcoming project, Moses had to come out of the desert before he could be used of God. Moses had to be flexible with all the challenges that confronted him and be willing to adjust to fit the need of leading his people out of captivity. It was a tremendous project to manage the exile of millions of people out of captivity in Egypt. He was the leader who led this project. He was responsible for the health and welfare of all the people, and when he came across a stumbling block, he simply crossed it. God made the way as He parted the waters and Moses led the way as the people crossed.

Quite often the project manager is faced with challenges to make modifications that will ultimately overcome those

If GOD doesn't build the house, the builders only build shacks. Psalms 127:1 (Message)

difficulties encountered that were not in the original design. As with a lot of projects, the end is not always as originally planned.

*John 21: 15-17* [15] *So when they had eaten breakfast, Jesus said to Simon Peter, "Simon, son of Jonah, do you love me more than these?" He said to Him, "Yes, Lord; You know that I love You." He said to him, "Feed My lambs."* [16] *He said to him again a second time, "Simon, son of Jonah, do you love me?" He said to Him, "Yes, Lord; You know that I love You." He said to him, "Tend My sheep."* [17] *He said to him the third time, "Simon, son of Jonah, do you love me?" Peter was grieved because He said to him the third time, "Do you love me?" and he said to Him, "Lord, You know all things; You know that I love You." Jesus said to him, "Feed My sheep.*

Jesus with His edifying nature was teaching Peter the significant role he and the other disciples had before them as pascere, shepherd. Obviously, Peter was upset that Jesus would ask him the same question three times. The first two times his response was, "You know that I love you." Jesus, though, posed the question three times to show the different stages the flock would encounter, and that the shepherd has a distinct responsibility at each level.

Jesus' response from the first question was to command Peter and us that we are to feed the lambs. Lambs are sheep that are less than a year old. It is no wonder that Jesus said "Suffer the little children to come unto me." In the second question, Jesus commands us to tend to the sheep, to care for and supervise them so they do not go astray. In the third question, Jesus commands

If God doesn't build the house, the builders only build shacks. Psalms 127:1 (Message)

~ Page 166 ~

that once we have taken care of their needs and guarded them, we are also to feed them the Word of God.

Jesus was trying to show Peter that, if we truly love Him, then we will love and take care of the flock the way He desires us to. It is in the third question that we need to find ourselves. Jesus knows every thought and intention of our heart even before we do and He wants us to love Him wholly so we can take care of the sheep entrusted to us.

This is where the project manager takes a lead role of redeeming the effort of the team. He bears the responsibility of assuring that the project does not digress from the original plan and that the subcontractors do not abandon the project because of frustration and discouragement. As people, we get our feelings hurt easily, and quite often we do not seem to react coherently. But we must learn to trust the project manager, as he is directed by God.

*Matthew 9:35-38, [35] Then Jesus went about all the cities and villages, teaching in their synagogues, preaching the gospel of the kingdom, and healing every sickness and every disease among the people. [36] But when He saw the multitudes, He was moved with compassion for them, because they were weary and scattered, like sheep having no shepherd. [37] Then He said to His disciples, "The harvest truly is plentiful, but the laborers are few. [38] therefore pray the Lord of the harvest to send out laborers into His harvest."*

A lost sheep separated from the flock will wander around in a state of confusion, unrest, and fear. It needs a shepherd to

If God doesn't build the house, the builders only build shacks. Psalms 127:1 (Message)

gather it home. When Jesus saw the multitude lost, profoundly perplexed, and confounded, He likened them to a sheep without a shepherd. Lost people are like lost sheep needing a shepherd to have compassion on them. God's plan was for us to emulate Jesus, the Good Shepherd, and become His project manager (local shepherd) of His construction project (sheep). Jesus' main concern is for the sheep to remain in the safety of the fold under the careful eye of the shepherd. Sheep make easy prey and become defenseless when they leave the fold, no matter the reason they leave. It could be that they do not feel adequate to fulfill their calling or that they feel there is no need for them because there are so many sheep. Most importantly, sheep leave when they take a wrong turn and no one is there to show the love that covers a multitude of sins.

One of the responsibilities that a project manager has is to make certain that all the safety rules imposed by OSHA are followed. It is not a hardship on the laborers to follow the rules for a construction site. It provides a hedge of protection around them from the dangers the project manager knows are out there. Pastors guard their spiritual sheep from going astray and defend them against the wiles of the enemy who is seeking to devour. The project manager has the great responsibility of overseeing not only the actual construction of a building, but also any person stepping foot on a jobsite. The building under construction is not the property of the project manager. He has been hired and entrusted by the owner to be sure the final product is as per the blueprints and ready to meet the occupant.

If GOD doesn't build the house, the builders only build shacks. Psalms 127:1 (Message)

# THE CONSTRUCTION PROJECT MANAGER

*Acts 20:28 Therefore take heed to yourselves and to all the flock, among which the Holy Spirit has made you overseers, to shepherd the church of God which He purchased with His own blood.*

If GOD doesn't build the house, the builders only build shacks. Psalms 127:1 (Message)

~ Page 169 ~

Chapter 12

# *Inspection and Conflict Management*

*Matt. 5:23-24 if your brother has something against you...go and be reconciled.*

$\mathcal{I}$t has been my experience over the years that things do not always go as planned in the construction process, so it is imperative that we maintain positive communication with the owner and municipalities. Builders, developers, owners and subcontractors must warrant that their work has been performed as per the plans and specifications approved by the reviewing agency.

Construction inspections are an essential part of the building process. Most municipalities employ building inspectors that will perform official on-site visits to confirm that the project under construction is adhering to federal, state, and local codes. In order to assure that the contractor is building the structure in compliance with the plans previously approved by the building official, inspections are performed at different stages during construction in order to protect the health and welfare of the public. It is almost certain that the building official (inspector), during his/her field inspection, will find some type of deficiency

If GOD doesn't build the house, the builders only build shacks. Psalms 127:1 (Message)

with the construction. This is primarily because no one is perfect and certain details on the plans can easily be overlooked. It can also result from a lack of communication or direction from the project manager. There may also be misunderstandings or even noncompliance of the local building codes. Quite often, I see contractors who are offended by the inspectors' disapproval of their work. The denial is considered a personal attack, and the disapproval creates friction with the inspector.

When we are faced with conflicts with another person, the ultimate goal is to resolve the problem by addressing it in the spirit of agreement instead of justifying our stance with proud arrogance. It is much easier to restore our relationship with the other person than to try to win our case. We must go before the Lord and examine our motives and allow the Lord to show us our shortcomings before dealing with the conflict. We need to make rational observations, not baseless accusations. We accomplish this by tending to the basic purpose behind the conflict and evaluating the things that need to happen, as opposed to pointing a finger or assaulting the other person's perspective, particularly if he is in a position of authority. Disagreements are a reality in the Christian life as in the construction process. What we must learn to do is to apply conflict management or conflict resolution throughout the construction process of the project. We may disagree with the city inspector, subcontractor, architect, project engineer, or perhaps even the suppliers.

I had a truckload of sheetrock delivered to my site, but unfortunately the truck was caught in a downpour and the materials got wet. It was my right to reject the materials, and I exercised that right. Immediately, this created conflict with the

If God doesn't build the house, the builders only build shacks. Psalms 127:1 (Message)

driver whose job was to deliver the materials. His office dispatched a manager who was very belligerent and insisted that I accept the materials. This man was a very large man; he was like a giant and I was like a grasshopper. Perhaps they sent him out as a form of intimidation. After asking that his company provide a guarantee that the sheetrock would not be faulty at a later time, he refused my request. He resorted to verbal abuse and threats. I called the police and had him and his materials removed from my property.

I realize that this case is an extreme example of a conflict, but what we must learn, though, is how to agree to disagree without anger, in a Christ-like, righteous manner. As a project manager, we are not representing ourselves, but the owner. In our Christian walk, we are not only representing ourselves, but we are also a testimony of the character of our Lord. If we are not careful, we could react to a denial or disapproval by others in such a way that it would be unbiblical and unhealthy. It could damage our personal witness and the other people we represent. We need to try to see the situation from the other person's perspective and understand that we are not perfect. There is always a compromise without offense. Some of us will not back down from a core belief, whether good or bad, and it drives us to choose an attack reaction instead of a thoughtful response. We have to learn to think before we respond.

I am reading a book written by Joel Osteen called, "I Declare," and in the introduction he tells a story of his efforts to renovate the Compaq Center in Houston. His architects gave him bad news that the project was going to cost millions more than they had estimated. In his mind, he formulated a response that it

If GOD doesn't build the house, the builders only build shacks. Psalms 127:1 (Message)

was going to be impossible to raise the additional money. He did not, however, verbalize what his mind was thinking. On the contrary, he declared a positive response with his mouth. We sometimes use arrogance and pride as weapons for winning a conflict rather than seeking to preserve a relationship. This type of behavior becomes a contest or an opportunity to affirm our rights, even if our thoughts are wrong. Our attempts to control others or take advantage of a situation will never give us the right to succeed at others expense. The inspector is the one person who controls the scheduled continuation of the project and any attempt to control or intimidate him will backfire.

Several years ago, I was building a house and the electrician was instructed to install a ground-fault circuit interrupter (GFCI) outlet behind the kitchen bar half-wall. Its purpose is to protect people from electrical shock, and it is installed in wet areas such as kitchens and bathrooms. While I respect the experience and knowledge of my subcontractors, I still follow closely behind them to check for quality of work. This electrician refused to place one in the specified place and argued that the building code did not require it. All the other electricians at my subdivision installed the GFCI outlets on similar houses without any persuading from me and without any argument, and the inspections passed the first time. I researched the code on the placement of the GFCI outlets and the wording was somewhat vague, so I assumed this electrician might have been correct. As I expected, however, the project did not pass the electrical inspection because of the absence of the GFCI outlet.

The electrician argued obstinately with the inspector. At this point, the inspector got irritated and lost confidence in the

If GOD doesn't build the house, the builders only build shacks. Psalms 127:1 (Message)

~ Page 173 ~

competence of the electrician, which impelled him to look meticulously at all the electrical work done on the project. The end result was that after vigorous evaluation of the work, the inspector required the electrician to redo some of the work, including installation of the GFCI outlet, which cost him additional time and money.

Because construction projects use flow charts to organize material delivery and start/stop dates for subcontractors, I tried to juggle moving schedules around, but the noncompliance of the electrician caused me a major delay. In the final analysis, if he would have been more cooperative and accommodating, the minor infraction could have been taken care of in 15 minutes. It was a minor point of contention, and his way was not the way to deal with the issue. As a result, it cost him a lot of extra work.

**Matthew 18:15-17,** *15 Moreover if your brother sins against you, go and tell him his fault between you and him alone. If he hears you, you have gained your brother. 16 But if he will not hear, take with you one or two more, that by the mouth of two or three witnesses every word may be established. 17 And if he refuses to hear them, tell it to the church. But if he refuses even to hear the church, let him be to you like a heathen and a tax collector.*

It always seems easier to avoid confrontation. Some have a tendency to shrink from it, fearing apprehension about how the other person will react. We are not certain if it will escalate to a greater level. Your approach may determine whether you will be welcomed or not.

If GOD doesn't build the house, the builders only build shacks. Psalms 127:1 (Message)

# INSPECTION AND CONFLICT MANAGEMENT

Disputes need to be resolved through peacemaking methods; however there may be times where neither party is amicable to the resolution being offered by the other party. It is at this point that outside or assisted intervention needs to take place from either the church or the community.

A mediation mechanism has been provided in the Word, so that if someone has erred against you, it can easily apply any time a conflict arises. Such a mechanism is to recruit other people that can help with an open dialog and explore possible resolutions.

There are times in business relationships where arbitration is required and a mediator will render a binding judgment to settle the matter. The purpose of arbitration is to give an unbiased determination of the issue, similar to a judge or jury that has inconsequential interest of either party. But even when we use the Biblical guideline in Matthew 18, there is the possibility of an irreconcilable breach. Our responsibility as the Body of Christ, as inspectors through conflict management, is to apply what we know is right in the Word, and leave the rest to God.

*Acts 15:36-41, [36] then after some days Paul said to Barnabas, "Let us now go back and visit our brethren in every city where we have preached the word of the Lord, and see how they are doing." [37] Now Barnabas was determined to take with them John called Mark. [38] But Paul insisted that they should not take with them the one who had departed from them in Pamphylia, and had not gone with them to the work. [39] Then the*

If GOD doesn't build the house, the builders only build shacks. Psalms 127:1 (Message)

~ Page 175 ~

*contention became so sharp that they parted from one another. And so Barnabas took Mark and sailed to Cyprus; ⁴⁰ but Paul chose Silas and departed, being commended by the brethren to the grace of God. ⁴¹ And he went through Syria and Cilicia, strengthening the churches.*

God is concerned about every area of our lives and as illustrated in the Bible, there are examples of common, normal, men to show us real life situations. Consider the story of Paul and Barnabas as it applies to working relationships within the church and/or a construction site. They were on a missionary journey working together accomplishing great things for God. But, as is common to man, a disagreement arose. Paul and Barnabas needed help in their ministry and Barnabas wanted his nephew John Mark to be involved again. The only issue is that John Mark, on their previous journey, had left from them to return to his home in Jerusalem. It is conceivable that Paul felt that he would leave them again on this second missionary trip and, consequently, he had no confidence in John Mark. A sharp contention arose among them.

The dissent between these two spiritual giants was not about any doctrinal matters, but simply a personal point of contention regarding a third party. Paul may have been guided by experience and reasoning, whereas Barnabas was moved perhaps by a warm heart. After all, Barnabas' name means "son of consolation." Might it be that Paul overlooked his own particular past and the grace extended to him? Proverbs 19:11, "A man's wisdom gives him patience; it is to his glory to overlook an offense."

If GOD doesn't build the house, the builders only build shacks. Psalms 127:1 (Message)

~ Page 176 ~

# INSPECTION AND CONFLICT MANAGEMENT

Tempers flared and no mediation was sought. They parted ways, but God's work was accomplished in spite of their differences. Perhaps God wanted John Mark to be brought back in for a second chance all along, but He desired for Paul and Barnabas to express Godly conflict management and work things out. In the end, John Mark proved himself and Paul later called for him. God's ministry flourished. The separation of their work did not upset the love and respect that they preserved for each other, and Paul mentioned that Barnabas was worthy of financial support in his ministry. One would think such an open conflict between such spiritual giants would not be recorded in the scriptures. The fact of the matter is that the Lord wants us to recognize that we will face conflicts in the work environment and with the church family, and we need to learn to resolve our differences for a higher service.

Most problems between Christians (the inspector, vendors and the subcontractors) appear as personal attacks (the inspector is out to get me or we are doing something that offends him); personality clashes (the inspector just "rubs you the wrong way"); and methodology differences (you do not agree with how they are interpreting the code book). Though you may be right theoretically, you may yet be sinning in the way you use your view to relate to your brother or sister (the inspector). Our objective in any relational conflict is not to win or to put the other person in his place. Our goal is to honor Christ by growing in maturity and by helping our brother or sister grow in maturity through the resolution conflict in line with Biblical truth.

If GOD doesn't build the house, the builders only build shacks. Psalms 127:1 (Message)

~ Page 177 ~

# INSPECTION AND CONFLICT MANAGEMENT

*Colossians 3:13 (NKJV) Bearing with one another, and forgiving one another, if anyone has a complaint against another; even as Christ forgave you, so you also must do.*

*Ephesians 4:26 (NKJV) "Be angry, and do not sin": do not let the sun go down on your wrath,*

*Matthew 5:9 (NKJV) blessed are the peacemakers, for they shall be called sons of God*

*Matthew 5:24 (NKJV) Leave your gift there before the altar, and go your way. First be reconciled to your brother, and then come and offer your gift.*

There are so many scriptures that teach us how to forgive the infractions of others and how to deal with the ones we commit. In our moment of weakness or perhaps stubbornness, however, we will separate ourselves from our instructions in the Word, and we can become angry and bitter toward those in the conflict. But I believe and I am learning that there is no conflict or problem that is too big to resolve with God and the other party. Conflict resolution is a way to draw closer to the other person and to glorify God. It allows us to show God's wisdom, care, and love even though we have an issue or a personality clash. You can almost be certain that sometimes, by design, someone will be sent our way to allow us to work on our rough edges.

Proverbs 27:17 tell us that, "*As* iron sharpens iron, so a man sharpens the countenance of his friend." The friction will eventually produce a smooth surface. In the body of Christ, we all

If GOD doesn't build the house, the builders only build shacks. Psalms 127:1 (Message)

~ Page 178 ~

need to learn to avow one another's strengths. God gives us differing personalities, ideas and gifts and we need to be diligent to safeguard the unity of the Spirit in the bond of peace. We are going to face plenty of disagreements in the church, or in a construction project. We have the challenge and opportunity to deal with our disagreements honorably and humbly. We know that Jesus not only makes all the difference in how we handle conflict but He will be glorified in it. The inspector may find a weakness in our construction, but with him and God's grace, the outcome of the final product will be as it was originally designed.

If GOD doesn't build the house, the builders only build shacks. Psalms 127:1 (Message)

~ Page 179 ~

Chapter 13

## *The Habitation*

*1Cor 12: ²⁰ But now indeed there are many members, yet one body. ²¹ And the eye cannot say to the hand, "I have no need of you"; nor again the head to the feet, "I have no need of you." ²² No, much rather, those members of the body which seem to be weaker are necessary. ²³ And those members of the body which we think to be less honorable, on these we bestow greater honor; and our unpresentable parts have greater modesty, ²⁴ but our presentable parts have no need. But God composed the body, having given greater honor to that part which lacks it, ²⁵ that there should be no schism in the body, but that the members should have the same care for one another. ²⁶ And if one member suffers, all the members suffer with it; or if one member is honored, all the members rejoice with it.*

The church is not the edifice in which we assemble, but rather it is the people in it that bring compassion, forgiveness, and healing to each other and to the world. The reason for the church is to help people understand a sound association with God and to acquaint the world with Jesus. So the church is a family where spiritual brothers and sisters are connected together with a common goal: allowing God to help us become more like Jesus. One thing is certain: we will spend eternity with the people around

If GOD doesn't build the house, the builders only build shacks. Psalms 127:1 (Message)

~ Page 180 ~

us that are in our circle of fellowship. We should get to know each other and share our friendship, compassion and love for one another. During this short time here on Earth, we need to prepare for an eternal relationship with each other, and the church is the place to develop a level of relationships that cannot be found anywhere else.

Consider the fact that there are many social clubs where people care about each other and have a common goal. The major difference between a social club and the church is that in the church, we are a family that **takes care** of each other and meets the spiritual, physical, and social needs of each member. I find it interesting that in 1 Corinthians 12, the only requirement for membership is to be part of the body and become a member one to another. A noteworthy contrast between a social club and the congregation is that in the Body of Christ, one part feels the agonies and praises the delight of other members.

In the event that my mouth develops a toothache, there is no doubt that my head (another individual member from the body) will build up a cerebral pain. It agonizes and identifies with the pain the other member is experiencing. In the construction of a structure, one out-of-place column will cause the beams and other members to feel the deficiency and the tremendous stress. On the other hand, if I get great news about something, my heart will rejoice and may cause my feet to become happy, my arms to be raised, my lips to move in praise, and my legs to jump up and down in celebration. As mentioned earlier, every member of a structure has an influence on the other members. All the members of the body will react for one another. In the construction process, you will not see a column jumping up and

If GOD doesn't build the house, the builders only build shacks. Psalms 127:1 (Message)

down, nor the foundation dancing around with happy feet. But the beauty of it is that we, the interior recipients, will trigger a joyful noise and activity that resonates through the very structure that is constructed with bricks and sticks. The church is a habitation, a sanctuary, a building, a place to express joy and bring sorrow.

The church body can congregate anywhere; inside in any heated and cooled space, outside under a large tent, in a storefront of a shopping center, in a home, inside a theater, in a gymnasium of a local public school or, as is the most common, a church building. Over time, there have been changing views and developments of the role of the building, its architectural style, and even the decorations of the interior of the church house. These progressions clearly mirror the nearby manufacturers' abilities, development strategies, new materials, social standards, and compositional conventions and advancements. In the book of Acts, however, we find Paul addressing the people of Athens, who have become very religious and confused about the God that they serve. He found an inscription on an altar "TO UKNOWN GOD." Paul makes the following proclamation to them:

*Acts 17:24* [24] *The God who made the world and everything in it is the Lord of heaven and earth and does not live in temples built by human hands.* [25] *And he is not served by human hands, as if he needed anything.*

Even if we build with the most sophisticated construction equipment, the most expensive materials, and take the most

If GOD doesn't build the house, the builders only build shacks. Psalms 127:1 (Message)

precise measurements, and use the latest technology, God may not choose to live there. He is not interested in a dwelling, in an edifice built by the hands of man, or a temple built of bricks and stick. He will inhabit the praises of his people. In the book of Exodus, the dwelling house of God was called the tabernacle. The tabernacle of the Old Testament was a "tent," a sacred place where God chose to meet His people during their 40 years in the wilderness. It was mobile, with furniture, and it was erected in the center of wherever they stopped to set up camp.

*Exodus 25:9 (KJV) According to all that I shew thee, after the pattern of the tabernacle, and the pattern of all the instruments thereof, even so shall ye make it.*

Although it may have been a tent, it had a very specific layout and detailed dimensions, including the size of each component and the type of construction materials. Oftentimes, there are so many dimensions shown on a set of construction plans that some may seem insignificant. But they have purpose and meaning, and they represent something that we may not understand. The designers placed them there for a reason. In the construction of the tabernacle where God would dwell, the details were very intricate. The outer court and the Holy of Holies measured 50 cubits wide by 100 cubits long. The gate to the outer court measured 20 cubits, and the altar of burnt offering measured 5 cubits by 5 cubits by 3 cubits high. The Holy place measured 10 cubits wide by 20 cubits long and the Holy of Holies had dimensions of 10 cubits wide by 10 cubits deep and 10 cubits high. As you can see, they were very detailed, they were

If GOD doesn't build the house, the builders only build shacks. Psalms 127:1 (Message)

accurately defined, and they were to be constructed with the same level of care and precision as a high-rise building.

*Exodus 35:30-35 ³⁰ And Moses said to the children of Israel, "See, the Lord has called by name Bezalel the son of Uri, the son of Hur, of the tribe of Judah; ³¹ and He has filled him with the Spirit of God, in wisdom and understanding, in knowledge and all manner of workmanship, ³² to design artistic works, to work in gold and silver and bronze, ³³ in cutting jewels for setting, in carving wood, and to work in all manner of artistic workmanship. ³⁴ "And He has put in his heart the ability to teach, in him and Aholiab the son of Ahisamach, of the tribe of Dan. ³⁵ He has filled them with skill to do all manner of work of the engraver and the designer and the tapestry maker, in blue, purple, and scarlet thread, and fine linen, and of the weaver— those who do every work and those who design artistic works.*

In the Old Covenant, Israel was called by God and formed into "God's Chosen People." The precise blueprint included detailed positions and skilled craftsmen specifically gifted in their workmanship. Engravers, tapestry makers, and other craftsmen were all necessary to build the "dwelling" of God.

*Ephesians 4:16 ¹⁶ from whom the whole body, joined and knit together by what every joint supplies, according to the effective working by which every part does its share, causes growth of the body for the edifying of itself in love.*

If GOD doesn't build the house, the builders only build shacks. Psalms 127:1 (Message)

When the "New Covenant" began, there were no plans with specific dimensions or designs given, and there was no divine command as to the type of materials to be used for construction. The edifice built by the hands of man was no longer significant. Instead, now the workers are to build an eternal home, one of the spirit.

The word "CHURCH" is from the New Testament word "EKKLESIA." It is a composite word that can be subdivided to "ek" which means out, and "klesis" meaning a calling, hence the idea of "being called out." We are called to be saints, sanctified for service to the body of Christ. We are not to be a disconnected, fragmented body of individuals, but a harmonious group that together forms a melodic symphony. We are to attract the world and draw them to the habitation of the King of Kings. The habitation, when we meet together in unison, should create a sweet aroma and a melodious sound that draws down the Kingdom of Heaven to our very presence. But we are called out to take a message of redemption beyond the four walls of the habitation. How beautiful are the feet of those of us that choose to proclaim the gospel of peace to this messed up and confused world. How beautiful are the feet of those that bring glad tidings of good news: news of hope, whose name is Jesus.

In the earlier chapters, I have depicted that there are many components that come together to form the structure of a building.

***Act 2:44 44 now all who believed were together, and had all things in common, 45 and sold their possessions and goods, and divided them among all, as anyone had need.***

If GOD doesn't build the house, the builders only build shacks. Psalms 127:1 (Message)

*⁴⁶ So continuing daily with one accord in the temple, and breaking bread from house to house, they ate their food with gladness and simplicity of heart, ⁴⁷ praising God and having favor with all the people. And the Lord added to the church daily those who were being saved.*

The early Church met in the synagogue daily as they were accustomed to doing, but they understood the value of "small groups." They went from house to house, breaking bread, remembering the death of the Lord and the blood shed on their behalf. The new church promoted fellowship and prayer through a community of homes, encouraging each other as individual links creating a strong chain. The early church experienced intense persecution by the Romans, particularly Nero, who was emperor when Peter and Paul were martyred. Even today, there are places in the world where the church is persecuted, but these congregations thrive underground, because they realize it is far more worthwhile to serve the risen King than to fear an earthly one. Just recently, a tormentor entered a local college and placed a gun on the head of the students gathered in a classroom and asked, "Are you a Christian?" Those that answered an undeniable "yes" with great conviction understood that God dwells within them, and that their habitation will be with Him for all eternity.

The Bible, while showing a few examples of the early church, does not give any guidelines for establishing churches. The Bible is clear, though, on the activities of the body when its people gather together in one place.

If GOD doesn't build the house, the builders only build shacks. Psalms 127:1 (Message)

A few examples are:

## *Reading and Exhortation* –

*1 Timothy 4:13 ¹³ Till I come, give attention to reading, to exhortation, to doctrine.*

The designers place a great deal of information on the plans and specifications that are given to the contractor, and the construction crews. These instructions are to be followed based on the integrity of all the calculations that designer performed. The reading and exhortation is the only manna that we have from heaven. This is our source of energy that is anointed by the Holy Spirit, and it will sustain us. Without it, it is certain that we will perish. Without coming together and studying its doctrine we will be tossed around like a reed in the wind, and no edifice in this world with its grand beams or its rigid supporting columns will give us the support we need. As they prepare the plans of a building, the engineers a usually have a weekly project managers' meeting to compare, study, and plan so they can be certain that they are doctrinally following the same objective.

## *Preach* –

*2 Timothy 4:2 ² Preach the word! Be ready in season and out of season. Convince, rebuke, exhort, with all longsuffering and teaching.*

Preaching is a proclamation, and many preachers have used construction terms for their audiences because they knew

If GOD doesn't build the house, the builders only build shacks. Psalms 127:1 (Message)

~ Page 187 ~

the audience would be familiar with these terms. The cornerstone was the principal stone placed at the corner of a building and was usually the most solid. Jesus is the Cornerstone that His church is to be built upon. He preached the Word and used construction metaphors. Isaiah and Amos used construction terminology like "measuring line and plumb line" to make their point because these were terms that the people would understand. Paul preached that we are no longer foreigners and aliens, but fellow citizens with God's people and members of God's household, built on the foundation of the apostles and prophets. The rock, stone, and foundation are structural terms utilized as a part of the outline and development of the building. Together, these make up the sanctuary and, as we might see, the exacting New Testament royal priesthood.

*1 Timothy 3:15 ¹⁵But if I am delayed, I write so that you may know how you ought to conduct yourself in the house of God, which is the church of the living God, the pillar and ground of the truth.*

The church is to proclaim our behavior. We do not first figure out how to behave in the world or in the economy of all the saved and then afterward apply those standards into the congregation. We are taught inside of the church how to conduct ourselves in the congregation and the world.

If GOD doesn't build the house, the builders only build shacks. Psalms 127:1 (Message)

## *Praise* –

Psalm 107:31-33, [31] Oh, that men would give thanks to the Lord for His goodness, and for His wonderful works to the children of men! [32] Let them exalt Him also in the assembly of the people, and praise Him in the company of the elders.

Oh how sweet it is to see brethren dwelling in unity, in one accord, of one mind, coming together to lift up Holy hands, and worship his majesty. Psalms tells us that even creation is commanded to praise God. When Jesus entered Jerusalem on Palm Sunday, the Pharisees rebuked the crowds that were praising Him. Jesus, however, said, "I tell you, that, if these should hold their peace, the stones would immediately cry out." I tell you that if we come into the edifice that we construct with our own hands but do not praise The Lord, the very rocks that were used in the concrete mix that were poured to form the foundation, the columns, the beams, the walls and even the roof will cry out and praise Him.

Habakkuk 2:11 for the stone shall cry out of the wall, and the beam out of the timber shall answer it.

So the question arises, how can inanimate objects cry out and praise Him? I must admit that my curiosity got the best of me, and I researched to try to understand how rocks can praise the Lord. I encourage you to study to show yourself approved.

If GOD doesn't build the house, the builders only build shacks. Psalms 127:1 (Message)

I found a number of articles from the North American Space Administration (NASA), Massachusetts Institute of Technology (MIT), and other studies that indicated that, although the sun lies 93 million miles away from the earth and the separation from our planet is in a vacuum, sound would not travel in a vacuum. Scientists, however, with the use of special equipment known as a Michelson Doppler Imager (MDI), are able to record acoustical wave patterns that produce a singing sound.

According to an article by In Worship (3) scientists have shown that there are specific frequencies that resonate from the sun's atmosphere. They say that when the sun shoots solar flares, sounds are emitted. The frequencies are too low for human ears to hear, so we can conclude that it is not singing for our ears to hear, but is singing to the Creator, and it is constant. These waves are similar to the study of the interior of the earth known as helioseismology. It is quite possible that with all the harmonic motion, and based on these resonating waves, that the earth is also praising the Lord.

*Luke 19:40, But He answered and said to them, "I tell you that if these should keep silent, the stones would immediately cry out."*

I do not know if this what the Bible was referring when it said **"the rocks will cry out."** All I know is that if the inanimate rocks can sing to the Lord, then I who am alive should cry out and worship and praise Him. In the 4<sup>th</sup> chapter of the book of Revelation, we find four creatures that spend day and night without a break crying out and worshiping Him, proclaiming

If GOD doesn't build the house, the builders only build shacks. Psalms 127:1 (Message)

~ Page 190 ~

"Holy, Holy, Holy, Lord God Almighty, who **was**, who **is**, and **is to come**." God has given us the privilege of praising Him, of tuning our voices while we are here in this world to worship him in His. If we do not, then creation will. I say: **Praise the Lord.** Today, praise and worship in our holy places is a multi-tactile movement, drawing in sights and sounds that usher people into the throne room.

For a worship service to take place, a large team of individuals must create the atmosphere to connect worshipers with each other and with God. In the church that I am a member of, we worship with a contemporary style of music, and there are a number of instrumentalist that harmoniously draw the congregation to the throne room of heaven. This composition of voices, together with instruments, is a key element in giving life and vitality to a worship service; a worship service that ultimately creates an inviting environment and encourages all to praise and worship in the architecture of the building. It becomes an environment that dispenses high energy throughout the room with a common cause to raise an anthem to the Lord. All its participants blend in harmony with a feeling that can inspire and magnify the message of the song. It opens up a new dimension of participation. Given these truths, it is essential that the church find ways to support and enhance its praise and worship service, and it needs to be done corporately.

There is a Biblical directive that should be as natural as breathing...to sing unto the Lord. Mary sang when her cousin Elizabeth hailed her as "favored." The radiant host sang at Jesus' introduction to the world. The blessed messengers sing around the throne of paradise. We must do likewise. Psalms 100 instructs

If GOD doesn't build the house, the builders only build shacks. Psalms 127:1 (Message)

us to make a joyful noise unto the Lord. That is a call for corporate worship. As soon as we enter the room with all its grandeur and furnishings, we should serve Him with gladness and come into his presence with singing. There is no greater place to enter into with thankfulness and break out into a praise service than in His house. But it is not the edifice with its vaulted ceilings, the ornamental columns, and the intricate mullions on the windows, the furnishings in the congregational room, the acoustics, the pews, the carpet, the sound system, the lighting, or even the pulpit that brings us into His presence.

Those are inanimate objects only used as tools. It is people calling down the Glory of God in unison that gives God a place to inhabit. Let us exalt him in the assembly of the people and remind ourselves that, if we do not praise him, then those inanimate objects will.

## *Tithes* –

*1 Corinthians 16:1-2, ¹ Now concerning the collection for the saints, as I have given orders to the churches of Galatia, so you must do also: ² On the first day of the week let each one of you lay something aside, storing up as he may prosper, that there be no collections when I come.*

We need to recognize that all our blessings come from the Lord. That includes our ability to work, which in turn allows us to make money. Everything that we possess is on loan from God. But when we look at ourselves as owners and not managers or stewards, we will view ourselves as self-sufficient. Imagine, for a moment, the structure of a building and particularly the roof. The

---

If GOD doesn't build the house, the builders only build shacks. Psalms 127:1 (Message)

roof has to be supported by walls or columns. Without them, it will not stand. The church (body) also has to be supported by those that attend where they are fed. It is a directive from the apostle Paul that on the first day of every week, we consistently lay something aside so that the resources will be there and it will not be necessary to take up a collection as special needs arise. These are the tithe and offerings that we are commanded to bring to the storehouse. At a minimum, we are to bring the tithe or first fruit.

Let us assume for a moment that the 10 percent tithe represents a 10,000-psi (pound per square inch) strength of concrete, and that the design criteria and specifications for a proposed building called for 10,000 psi for all structural components. If we only bring 5 percent or 5,000 psi concrete and pour that into the forms, when the concrete cures or hardens, it will only be able to carry a portion of the load that the designers designed it for. Consequently, we create a weakened structure, and the structure will fail. You may think that God does not need your money, but the fact of the matter is that you would not have that money if it were not for God.

It is very difficult to evangelize the world if the resources are not made available by the faithful bringing in the first fruit. While it is true that God can cause things to happen, He prefers cooperation with us here on planet earth, as in the example with Noah. God did not have to ask Noah to build the ark; He could have simply spoken it into existence. But I believe that God wants the participation of grateful people to be involved in the task. In Adams case God provided a garden with all its provision, but He still commissioned Adam to keep and guard the garden. Adam

If GOD doesn't build the house, the builders only build shacks. Psalms 127:1 (Message)

~ Page 193 ~

was to have an active role, as it is required that we have an active role in developing the Kingdom.

## *Chain of Command* –

*Corinthians 12:27-29, [27] now you are the body of Christ, and members individually. [28] And God has appointed these in the church:*

*first apostles, second prophets, third teachers, after that miracles, then gifts of healings, helps, administrations, varieties of tongues.*

In this verse, Paul is not suggesting that we do things in the church individually, doing our own thing, but that we have a very personal individual responsibility to the ministry that God has assigned to us. The fact of the matter is that we are all instructed to submit to one another, understanding that Christ is the head, or the leader of the church. Without the beams, the roof could not stand; without the column, the beam could not stand; and without the foundation, the column could not stand. We all have a unique calling in our service and we have to fulfill that service with everything that is within us and to help to support the rest of the body. We may be individual members, but like in a symphony, we assemble ourselves, and we are directed by the maestro, Jesus, to produce a wonderful stunning success. In our church environment, God has appointed and assigned a major responsibility to the pastor. He is the shepherd that will lead the flock. It is our responsibility that we undergird him so that the devil will not pull the carpet from under him.

If GOD doesn't build the house, the builders only build shacks. Psalms 127:1 (Message)

## *Healing* –

*Rom 12:4-5* *⁴ For as we have many members in one body, but all the members do not have the same function, ⁵ so we, being many, are one body in Christ, and individually member of one another.*

*James 5:13-14, ¹³ is anyone among you suffering? Let him pray. Is anyone cheerful? Let him sing psalms. ¹⁴ Is anyone among you sick?*

*Let him call for the elders of the church, and let them pray over him, anointing him with oil in the name of the Lord.*

The church is a habitation of people composed of many members who are inviting and cheerful, and who are rejoicing and singing psalms. If there are some sick among us, however, then the body of Christ should be hospitable. The word hospitable is defined as welcoming others with generosity, and being friendly. The word hospitable can be broken down as an "able hospital." The church body is a place where people should come to receive treatment for their illnesses.

I have a great respect for doctors. They have a high calling to mend broken bodies and prescribe medicines to assist our bodies in the healing process. As I mentioned previously, when adult onset Type II Diabetes changed my life, my doctor was prescribing and often times providing me with certain medicines needed for my healing. But the greatest medicine Dr. Jacob Gruel offered me was his caring and loving undivided attention. He was a hospitable man. No matter the backlog of sick people in the

If GOD doesn't build the house, the builders only build shacks. Psalms 127:1 (Message)

~ Page 195 ~

lobby waiting to receive his treatment, Dr. Jacob always took time to pray for me. There are many sick people in the world, and it could be that all they need is a hospitable place to show them as Proverbs 17:22, how a merry heart does well like a medicine. It may seem this portion of the scripture from James is out of place: *"Is anyone cheerful? Let him sing psalms."* But I believe James understood the church body can heal so many broken hearts, help so many burdened bodies, and ease minds in turmoil simply by being hospitable, loving, and cheerful.

If GOD doesn't build the house, the builders only build shacks. Psalms 127:1 (Message)

If GOD doesn't build the house, the builders only build shacks. Psalms 127:1 (Message)

**Chapter 14**

*The Finishing*

*Touches*

*Luke 12:16-21* *16 Then He spoke a parable to them, saying: "The ground of a certain rich man yielded plentifully. 17 And he thought within himself, saying, 'What shall I do, since I have no room to store my crops?' 18 So he said, 'I will do this: I will pull down my barns and build greater, and there I will store all my crops and my goods. 19 And I will say to my soul, 'Soul, you have many goods laid up for many years; take your ease; eat, drink, and be merry.'' 20 But God said to him, 'Fool! This night your soul will be required of you; then whose will those things be which you have provided?' 21 "So is he who lays up treasure for himself, and is not rich toward God."*

$\mathcal{I}$n our country as in many countries, it has become a mandate that, upon completing their secondary education, young people are to secure a well-paying job and invest in a retirement program, annuities, and stocks, all for the day that they will retire and merrily live a life of ease. There are countless principles in the word of God that advise us how to live our lives, but simply living in a state of perpetual rest is not one of those

If GOD doesn't build the house, the builders only build shacks. Psalms 127:1 (Message)

principles. When we develop the frame of mind that we have acquired all that there is, and it is time to sit back and enjoy (retire), God says we are fools, and that night our soul will be required of us.

We may think "I have worked my entire life and merit this," or that we doubtlessly deserve it. The problem arises when we have a wealth of time and money at our disposal, but we neglect the Kingdom of God. We may try to validate the retirement concept of doing nothing by using the scripture found in Numbers 8:25, where God instructs Moses that the Levites that are the age of 50 are to retire from regular service and work no longer.

Perhaps we reach a point where we become exhausted and essentially our feeble bodies do not have the natural strength to accomplish building God's house. Maybe our health has diminished, but the worst thing to do is to give up and think that there is nothing else to do that will matter, and turn out the light and give up. We cannot give up, and we cannot stop. We must move to the next verse that tells us that we can assist our brothers in performing their duties. In reality, God was never hindered in His plan by someone's age, only by his or her desire to serve Him.

Perhaps we cannot do things at the same pace and with the same energy level that we did when we were younger. But the wisdom gained in the experience of life should lead our hearts, our minds, and our willingness to still do great things for God. Childhood is a time of instruction, as we are given direction from our parents; a time where we can grow strong and confident and we are encouraged by our family and those caring adults that want to make a difference in our lives. Middle age is a time of

If GOD doesn't build the house, the builders only build shacks. Psalms 127:1 (Message)

human adulthood that promptly goes before the onset of maturity. It is a time of intelligence and gathering of knowledge; it is a time of wisdom not only from learned knowledge, but also from the school of experiencing life and its lessons. True wisdom is not from our intellect, but from a full heart gained from a journey of steps taken while walking with the Lord.

Consider a church building constructed today: our emphasis would begin with the intent of the building being constructed. We would speak about the call of God and emphasize the vision and the great commission for His church in the community and the world. The books of Ezra, Nehemiah, and Ester share the story of the freedom from captivity for the Jews. They were allowed to return home to rebuild the one place they believed God inhabited. Ezra begins with the building of the temple. The restoration of the house then comes with the building of the walls, as in the book of Nehemiah. Nehemiah did more than rebuild a wall with bricks and sticks; he penned the story of the restoration of a people from devastation and despair to a new walk with God.

Jerusalem was not only a historic city, but also a symbolic one. Jerusalem is also used in a pictorial sense throughout the Scriptures, representing the place where God desires to dwell. At the point when the city was initially assigned to King David as the spot where God needed him to assemble the sanctuary, he was informed that this was the spot where God would stay among his kin. It was only a representation, however, of where God would be. The actual place where God wants to dwell is in the heart of man. God's plan was for the Holy Spirit to dwell in the human spirit. The story of how our local church was born would not start

If GOD doesn't build the house, the builders only build shacks. Psalms 127:1 (Message)

out with the design plans, materials, construction process, or the dedication of the building. The story would originate with the family God called, gathered, and ordained. It may have its roots in the garage of someone's house, in a school gym or perhaps in the back of a warehouse building.

The book of Esther reveals the purpose of the life of any individual. The story actually happens when God begins to move in the midst of Israel's seventy years of captivity. God raised Esther, a young Jewish woman, to the throne of Persia as queen. She had been placed in this prominent position by the grace of God. Esther was sent to move the heart of her husband, the Persian king, Ahasuerus, thought to be the emperor Xerxes. It was this king that would allow Nehemiah, his cupbearer, to return to Jerusalem. Nehemiah started the work of modifying the city of Jerusalem. Some quarter of a century later, Zerubbabel came back with around 50,000 of the hostages from Babylon, as is recorded in the book of Ezra.

As I get older, I find it interesting that the things I value the most are memories of family, friends, and impacting other peoples' lives. Even now, as I am going through a transition phase, I find myself lifting my heart toward heaven wondering what I can do for God. Reaching the age of senior adult does not mean an end to a fruitful life. You may feel that because you are in your last years and your knees buckle and your eyesight is waning that there is no ministry for you. The excitement of your day may be picking up your prescriptions from the pharmacy. But you bring them home to an empty house with a large medicine cabinet.

If GOD doesn't build the house, the builders only build shacks. Psalms 127:1 (Message)

God does not see physical death as the end; it is simply the final season of life on earth. The most damaging belief for an elderly person is to feel there is nothing left for them to do, except die. The following examples are people just like us that decided to do something great or just something that had been a desire for a long time. It required an intentional decision to make a goal and reach it.

This book was birthed in me over 10 years ago. A number of inventions that I have, were born on a mission trip to the Dominican Republic along the Haiti border that are only now beginning to take form. Although I may be getting up in years, I still have the vision of the inventions as the first day He placed the ideas in my head. I may be getting older, but He is not finished with me. There is a lot more for me to do under my sun, and more important for **His Son**.

## *Here are some finishers:*

60 years old - The playwright **George Bernard Shaw** finished writing his masterpiece "Heartbreak House."

62 years old - **J.R.R. Tolkien** published the first volume of his fantasy series, "Lord of the Rings."

65 years old - **Harlan David Sanders**, aka Colonel Sanders, founded the Kentucky Fried Chicken Company.

65 years old - **Miles Davis** performed his final live jazz album weeks before he died.

66 years old - **Noah Webster** completed his monumental "American Dictionary of the English Language."

If GOD doesn't build the house, the builders only build shacks. Psalms 127:1 (Message)

70 years old - **Cornelius Vanderbilt** began buying railroads.

72 years old - **Margaret Ringenberg** flew around the world.

73 years old – **Peter Mark Roget** designed a scientific order of language consisting of a system of classifying words that had similar definition...the Thesaurus.

76 years old - **Anna Mary Robertson Moses**, aka Grandma Moses, could no longer embroider due to painful arthritis so she began painting and did so until she died at 101.

81 years old - **Benjamin Franklin** affected the compromise that led to the adoption of the U.S. Constitution.

83 years old - famed baby doctor **Benjamin Spock** championed for world peace.

89 years old - **Arthur Rubinstein** performed one of his greatest recitals in Carnegie Hall.

92 years old - **Paul Spangler** ran and finished his 14th marathon.

95 years old - **Nola Ochs** became the oldest person to receive a college diploma.

96 years old - **Harry Bernstein** published his first book, "The Invisible Wall," to divert loneliness of losing his wife of 67 years, Ruby. He published his second book a year later, his third in one more year and his fourth was published a year after he died at age 101.

97 years old - **Martin Miller** was still working fulltime as a lobbyist on behalf of benefits for seniors.

If GOD doesn't build the house, the builders only build shacks. Psalms 127:1 (Message)

As we grow older, we are to remain planted in the house of the Lord, deeply rooted and flourishing. The aging among us must not be viewed as a bunch of dried up 2 x 4 boards that are simply taking up space in the church. We may retire from working a secular job, but there is no such thing as retirement from serving our churches, the people in our communities nor our God. Look at how Psalms show the sovereignty of God in the enduring fruitful life of the righteous.

*Psalm 92:12-15, ¹²the righteous shall flourish like a palm tree, He shall grow like a cedar in Lebanon. ¹³Those who are planted in the house of the LORD shall flourish in the courts of our God.*

*¹⁴They shall still bear fruit in old age; they shall be fresh and flourishing, ¹⁵to declare that the LORD is upright; He is my rock, and there is no unrighteousness in Him.*

*Psalms 71:17-18, ¹⁷O God, You have taught me from my youth; and to this day I declare Your wondrous works. ¹⁸Now also when I am old and gray headed, O God, do not forsake me, until I declare Your strength to this generation, Your power to everyone who is to come.*

There are also numerous Biblical examples of those that began ministry late in life. Lessons learned from life are priceless and sometimes we are not capable to use them until we become mature (old), and God allows us.

---

If GOD doesn't build the house, the builders only build shacks. Psalms 127:1 (Message)

*For instance:*

75 years old - **Abraham** was called by God to leave his country to begin a new life in a strange land.

80 years old - **Moses** was called to go before Pharaoh.

83 years old - **Aaron** became a spokesman for Moses

91 years old – **Anna**, a prophetess, served God with fasting and praying night and day.

100 years old - **Abraham** and his 90-year-old wife **Sarah** became parents to the first Hebrew descendent.

God stressed the importance reaching a point of maturity, a point at which the building is guaranteed to stand. The job of the elderly within the church is as important as any other component, and the structure is weakened when they do not fulfill their purpose.

*Titus 2:1-8 ¹But as for you, speak the things which are proper for sound doctrine: ²that the older men be sober, reverent, temperate, sound in faith, in love, in patience; ³the older women likewise, that they be reverent in behavior, not slanderers, not given to much wine, teachers of good things— ⁴that they admonish the young women to love their husbands, to love their children, ⁵to be discreet, chaste, homemakers, good, obedient to their own husbands, that the word of God may not be blasphemed. ⁶Likewise, exhort the young men to be sober-minded, ⁷in all things showing yourself to be a pattern of good works; in doctrine showing integrity, reverence, incorruptibility, ⁸sound speech that cannot be condemned, that one who is an opponent may be ashamed, having nothing evil to say of you.*

If GOD doesn't build the house, the builders only build shacks. Psalms 127:1 (Message)

This verse actually demonstrates God's plan for the church to function as a single unit...a family unit. Every level of the building leads to the strength of the whole. The generational gap, which is not Biblical, needs to be closed. To get a blessing, young people should visit the elderly in this church; talk to them and listen to them. They have an abundance of knowledge and experience that is established in a profound association with Jesus Christ. They might have reached a ripe old age, but they have lots of fruit they want to share coming from a tree rooted in a life of walking with Jesus.

*Jesus loves me, this I know,*
*Though my hair is white as snow;*
*Though my sight is growing dim,*
*Still He bids me trust in Him.*
*Yes, Jesus loves me,*
*Yes Jesus loves me,*
*Yes, Jesus loves me,*
*The Bible tells me so.*
*Though my steps are, oh, so slow*
*With my hand in His I'll go*
*On through life; let come what may,*
*He'll be there to lead the way.*

If GOD doesn't build the house, the builders only build shacks. Psalms 127:1 (Message)

~ Page 206 ~

*When the nights are dark and long,*
*In my heart He puts a song,*
*Telling me in words so clear,*
*"Have no fear for I am near."*
*When my work on earth is done*
*And life's victories' been won*
*He will take me home above*
*To the fullness of His love.*

C.D. Frey, Tennessee, in <u>The Bible Friend</u>.

Buildings wear out and at times need restoration. There will be a time when they will fall on their own or from a planned demolition, allowing for a new building to be reconstructed on the same site. The one advantage is that there is already history about the site that will inform the new builders of deficiencies. If there were mistakes made in the past, God has made a way for restoration. The same pitfalls should not be repeated again. The book of Nehemiah gives the background of the rebuilding of the walls of Jerusalem. In our lives, the rebuilding of the walls would be an illustration of re-establishing the strength that difficulties in life may have taken from us.

It is not uncommon to allow our defenses to crumble away. We become humanly dilapidated, weakened, helpless, and sometimes absolutely hopeless. We lose perspective and launch ourselves into discouragement.

---

If GOD doesn't build the house, the builders only build shacks. Psalms 127:1 (Message)

A story is told about Oxford University founded in 1379. The university has a dining hall with massive oak beams that not only adorn the dining hall but are the structural support for the roof above. The massive beams are 2 feet by 2 feet by 45 feet long each. It was discovered that the beams were infested by beetles, which corrupted the structural integrity of the beams. The college council wanted to maintain the harmony with the rest of the beams by the same materials as the original. The problem was that it was nearly impossible to find such size beams.

When the college was founded, the forefathers anticipated this day might come and they made provisions. They planted a grove of oak trees on the campus grounds. To the average person, they were normal oak trees, but to the foresters who maintained this grove, they were the future. It was passed on from forester to forester that those oak trees were not to be cut down, for they had a greater purpose. Ultimately, while the story is mythical, the emphasis is to plan ahead for the future. The emphasis would be on the vision and the great commission for the church in the community and the world. We are to leave a legacy that will be passed on from generation to generation until the Lord returns. God, in His grace, frequently reaches down, brings us out, and fortifies us to rebuild the walls.

If GOD doesn't build the house, the builders only build shacks. Psalms 127:1 (Message)

When we build,
Let us know that we build to last.
Let it not be for present delight or for personal
gratification.
Let it be that our offspring will continue,
To establish the Kingdom.
Let us know that we lay a stone,
With Jesus being the Chief Corner Stone.
Let us build as a reminder,
Of the work of the hands of our fore fathers,
And let our offspring say
That we were a worthy example of,
Good and Faithful Servants.

2nd Timothy 2:15. Do your best to present yourself to God as one approved, a worker who does not need to be ashamed and who correctly handles the word of truth.

If GOD doesn't build the house, the builders only build shacks. Psalms 127:1 (Message)

## Chapter 15

# *The Closeout*

*Ephesians 2:20-22, [20] having been built on the foundation of the apostles and prophets, Jesus Christ Himself being the chief cornerstone, [21] in whom the whole building, being fitted together, grows into a holy temple in the Lord, [22] in whom you also are being built together for a dwelling place of God in the Spirit.*

$\mathcal{T}$his book is but a snapshot of how the structure of any life, of any building, of any local church can be built into strength and power and purpose. I earnestly pray that the book has given you a new insight and has challenged you to study the Word of God with a deep sense of examination of its truth revealed to you relative to your gifting's. For me, it has been through engineering, using mathematics and science. For some, it may be through finances, using mathematics and statistics, or perhaps as a counselor using the psyche of man. Perhaps your talent is music, and the book of Psalms resonates with you. Your gift and talent

If GOD doesn't build the house, the builders only build shacks. Psalms 127:1 (Message)

may involve the media of a church, and you may identify with the book of Revelation or the books of the Major Prophets with their forward and back flashes of time and abstract representations. Whatever the case, allow the Holy Spirit to help you study to show yourself approved.

I hope that you were able to get a glimpse of simple, basic principles of engineering and construction as they relate to the Kingdom of God, and how the supernatural principles from the Word can be applied to our lives in our natural world.

We began this journey by indicating how God made us unique and provided us with an instructional manual to follow, and a Holy Spirit to guide us through our lives by using the metaphor of the construction of a building. The Word contains the comprehensive plans and specifications that are needed to construct a life, a career, a business, a family, a marriage, a home, and His church.

Throughout the book, it has been shown that we are one member of a body composed of many members, and that we need to work together to accomplish God's plan for our lives. Considering the size of our world and the complexity within individuals, it is, at times, impossible to achieve a close-knit community. Regardless, we are all members of the church proclaiming God's love to everyone as children of the one, true God. With all the intricacies of the construction of a building, the mathematical equations, and the scientific knowledge, and even with all Biblical knowledge, if love is not applied, then it is a hollow symbol of Christianity, as expressed in the following poem by Rebekah B. Marsh.

If GOD doesn't build the house, the builders only build shacks. Psalms 127:1 (Message)

# The Church Construction Paraphrase of 1st Corinthians 13

Though we speak with the tongues of men and of angels about
Church growth and plans for expansion, but make no plans for building
A climate of love, caring, and spiritual growth for our people,
Our plans will be empty and any building erected will be only
A hollow symbol of Christianity.

Though we have faith to believe God will move his people to
Provide the necessary funds, yet do not love and trust each other,
Our efforts will be fruitless, and though we bestow much money,
And sacrifice personal luxuries for concrete and mortar, without love,
We will be adding nothing to our treasures in the kingdom of heaven.

Building a climate of love and unity takes time and patience.
Love deals kindly with everyone, no matter what his position in life.
Love leaves no room to envy the large churches others have built.
It will not blame others for the lack of vision and good planning.
It does not seek to carry out its own plans,
While laying the financial burden on others.

Love's motives are pure.
It tells the whole truth about the means of financing.
Love is patient while the building contractor makes an error.
It believes he really is trying to do his best.

Love endures to the end of the project,
Seeing each detail completed.

If GOD doesn't build the house, the builders only build shacks. Psalms 127:1 (Message)

Believers working together in love and unity
Will produce far more than a building.
For buildings serve their purpose and one day crumble.
Yet the fruit of love is harmony and spiritual growth,
And redemption for unbelievers.

Our insight into God's plan for a building will change.
For we know in part and plan in part.

But when the end of the age comes and we see God's great plan,
We will understand all He has in mind for us.
For the present, however, we plan in finite ways
Because we are only human,
With human understanding and limitations.

Now there abides faith to go ahead with our expansion project,
Hope that God will guide and give wisdom,
And love-a caring, climate in which we can carry on his work.

But the greatest of these is love that
Unites believers in every endeavor,
Even building projects.

If GOD doesn't build the house, the builders only build shacks. Psalms 127:1 (Message)

# Author's Closing Comments:

*I*f you just finished reading this book, I want to thank you for your faithfulness to see it through, and if you have not started yet, I want to fill you in on the purpose. From the moment God put this book in my heart, it was always meant to be more than just a good read or an informative devotion. It was meant to be a catalyst for the growth of the Kingdom (spiritually and literally) around the world.

There is a higher purpose that the Lord has placed in my heart. Although He called me with a specific plan when I was a young man, it is disturbing to say that I am no different than the children of Israel were. I have learned a lot through the school of hard knocks, the result of a short journey that involved years of grief. The amazing thing is that I serve a loving, merciful God that was willing to seek after me in my wayward state. His goodness and mercy has followed me all the days of my life, and now I must be obedient, responsive and have the same heart of compassion for others that His son had for me, so that I may dwell in His house forever.

The Lord has placed certain talents, skills, and abilities in me that I am responsible and accountable for, and that I am to use in His ministry. My call is to provide our brothers and sisters in the world with some of the essentials needed for a heathy life. I have all the technology of sophisticated software programs that can provide the construction plans for an orphanage, a clinic, a school, and a place of worship, at my disposal.

If GOD doesn't build the house, the builders only build shacks. Psalms 127:1 (Message)

If your ministry is at the phase where you are ready to break ground, or you just have a picture in your head of a building that you see serving your ministry, I want to know how I can serve you. Solution Finders International (SFI) has been formed for the sole purpose of providing ministries without the budget to hire construction and design experts, with the tools needed to carry out the vision God has given to them. To find out more about me, and how we can co-labor together, visit us at www.sf.international or email me at jerry@sf.international I look forward to partnering with you to see His Kingdom come!

If GOD doesn't build the house, the builders only build shacks. Psalms 127:1 (Message)

~ Page 215 ~

# About the Author:

*J*erry was born in Costa Rica and his family moved to the United States when he was 10 years old. He grew up in New York City and soon after high school, joined the United States Air Force and worked in the engineering field. He is a fifth generation engineer/surveyor that has mathematics and science running through his veins. Jerry studied civil engineering with an emphasis in structural engineering, and has been in the engineering and surveying profession for over 40 years.

As a young man, his association with the Lord did not go any further than going to a religious service at a building where he put no energy in knowing Jesus. While serving in the Air Force in the civil engineering field, he encountered a period where the Lord was getting him ready for His calling. God, in His infinite grace, went as far as housing him in a dormitory wing where many of the airmen, except him, were believers in Christ. They shared the message of the love of Jesus with him and, like the apostle Paul, he persecuted the church in retaliation. He got inebriated on Saturday evenings, and then on Sunday, he went to a church and creates a scene. This process continued for quite some time. All the while, God in His mercy and leniency was seeking after Jerry. The airmen in his dorm continued to pester him to come to church with them until finally he agreed, just so that he could shut them up. As a form of compromise and with the hope that he would be left alone, he struck a deal with them that he would go one time, provided they left him alone thereafter. Jerry had never encountered the fullness of affection and acknowledgment that

If GOD doesn't build the house, the builders only build shacks. Psalms 127:1 (Message)

he received from the members of that congregation. After the pricking of his heart by the Holy Spirit, he surrendered his life to the Lord.

Before long, the Lord called Jerry to serve Him in the ministry. In the absence of comprehension, however, and with insistence from the Lord, Jerry served the Lord in what he accepted as his purpose in life. He served God in his own particular limits and with his own particular plans. Time and time again, the specific call was put over him, and God in His loving mercy did not pull back the calling put on Jerry.

Jerry has served the Lord in many capacities in church government, and has traveled abroad to many countries in Latin America as a short-term missionary. He has served in the capacity of a designer as well as a contractor, in addition to serving on youth trips and medical mission trips. The calling placed in his life is to serve the Lord in complete obedience to Him, using the tools and gifts that have been placed in His life: the tools of engineering, surveying, and construction, using his native language of Spanish. It is Jerry's conviction that, in the Kingdom of God, there are a multitude of members with diverse talents and abilities that can propel the kingdom in a significant manner.

He has composed this book with an end goal to show the Gospel's usefulness by means of engineering and construction methods. True wisdom is not in the intellect. Wisdom comes from our journey and learning along every step that we have taken with the Lord. Jerry's vision is to enrich the world with the truth of the Gospel and use the gifts and talents the Lord has placed in his life. From this vision, he is called to provide and equip the underdeveloped nations of this world with design and construction of facilities for the Kingdom of God.

If GOD doesn't build the house, the builders only build shacks. Psalms 127:1 (Message)

# Bibliography

Unless otherwise noted, all scripture taken from the New King James Version®. Copyright © 1982 by Thomas Nelson. Used by permission. All rights reserved.

Gregg, Aguirre. 2015 Capital Rivers Commercial. February 16.
Accessed November 18. 2015
http://www.capitalrivers.com/news/2015/2/16/what-if-noah-tried-to-build-the-ark-today

Dan, Graves. 2007. *Christianity.com*. June.
Accessed July 14, 2015
http://www.christianity.com/church/church-history/timeline/1801-1900/blind-louis-braille-gave-reading-to-the-blind-11630360.html

Carroll, Ray. 2013. *Fallen Pastor*. November 21. Accessed July 18, 2015.
http://fallenpastor.com/are-we-really-losing-1500-pastors-a-month/.

Trf, Brent. 2007. *inWorship*. April 21. Accessed July 14, 2015.
http://brenttrf.blogspot.com/2007/04/even-rocks-cry-out.html.

Shea, Benett. 2014. *Social Times*. November 10. Accessed August 18, 2015
http://www.adweek.com/socialtimes/social-media-minutes-day

Clarence, Larkin. 1920. *Dispensational Truth of God's Plan and Purpose in the ages*. Philadelphia: Sunnyside.

Osteen, Joel. 2012. *I Declare*. New York: Hatchette Book Group, Inc.

Trf, Brent. 2007. *inWorship*. April 21. Accessed July 14, 2015.
http://brenttrf.blogspot.com/2007/04/even-rocks-cry-out.html.

Boks, Ed. Unknown. *Feasibilty Studies*. Accessed June 8, 2015.
http://www.edboks.com/uploads/Feasibility_Studies Boks_Consulting.pdf.

If GOD doesn't build the house, the builders only build shacks. Psalms 127:1 (Message)

If GOD doesn't build the house, the builders only build shacks. Psalms 127:1 (Message)